for George
with thanks for your
friendship and your ministry

Frank Wade

BIBLICAL FRACKING

BIBLICAL FRACKING

Midrash for the Modern Christian

FRANCIS H. WADE

WIPF & STOCK · Eugene, Oregon

BIBLICAL FRACKING
Midrash for the Modern Christian

Wipf & Stock
An Imprint of Wipf and Stock Publishers
199 W. 8th Ave., Suite 3
Eugene, OR 97401

www.wipfandstock.com

PAPERBACK ISBN: 978-1-5326-7133-3
HARDCOVER ISBN: 978-1-5326-7134-0
EBOOK ISBN: 978-1-5326-7135-7

Manufactured in the U.S.A.   JUNE 4, 2019

For my special friends
Lila and Wade Greiner
and
Jackson, Kathryn, and Haden Wade

Contents

Acknowledgments

WHEN I PAUSE TO consider the people who have inspired, informed, and enabled this book I am, like the author of Hebrews, "surrounded by a great cloud of witnesses." I could never sort through the teachers, mentors, guides, and exemplars who laid the foundations of what I think of as imaginative scholarship. It is a little easier to identify those who have been prominent as a jumble of ideas began to coalesce into book form. The encouragement of Rev. Dr. Ian Markham, Dean and President of Virginia Theological Seminary in Alexandria, was and remains essential. The developmental support of my colleagues Rev. Dr. Melody Knowles, Dr. Tim Sedgwick, and Rev. Randy Alexander has been a great help while being great fun. Philip Kopper has been invaluable as an able editor, wise counselor, and faithful friend. Rev. Dr. Joseph Clark is my soul friend who helps me to better understand the fragile gift of life. My neighbors Hugh and Mary Jane Nugent blessed me with their thoughtful enthusiasm. And finally, my wife Kerry gave not only wise commentary and gentle encouragement, but is also the prime source of joy and wonder in my life upon which the business of fracking is utterly dependent.

Introduction

Biblical Fracking

EARLY IN OUR FAITH story, when oral tradition held sway over the written, our spiritual ancestors knew the necessity of going beyond repeating the ancient stories and began expounding on them. In doing so, they quickly found themselves in fascinating but uncharted waters. They knew about the garden and the serpent, but began to wonder why Adam did not stop Eve from eating the apple. They knew Abraham as an adult, but wondered what he was like as a child. Such speculation became the foundation of Jewish midrash, which means "seeking" and "inquiring." Its more modern interpretation is "to expound." The meanings come together as teaching based on wonder and inquiry. Speculation on biblical stories moved from the oral tradition to the written, making their way into the Dead Sea Scrolls and other treasures. The practice separated itself from interpretation of laws and practices (*midrash halakah*) and came to stand alone as reflection on stories (*midrash aggada*). Written collections, often contradictory and seldom conclusive, enriched the Jewish narratives, beginning in the first century BCE, and continue to do so today.

When Christians separated from Judaism, they took the basic mythologies as well as the Law and Prophets with them. But somehow, intentional midrash failed to convey in a similar way, so Christianity took shape without it. Perhaps the evangelical zeal of the early church coupled with the expectation that Christ was coming soon to end this world took precedence over the midrash invitation to wonder and wander in the rich stories handed down. It is difficult to imagine how Christianity might have been altered if its earliest practitioners had indulged in wider exploration beyond the written texts. While many spiritual disciplines use imagination, most notably the *Spiritual Exercises* of Ignatius Loyola, contemporary Christian "seeking" in the midrash sense has been mostly secular. In the 1940s, Lloyd C. Douglas wrote *The Robe*, a popular story about the soldier who won Jesus' garment at the crucifixion. Dorothy Sayers produced a series of radio plays titled *The Man Born to be King* that included fresh interpretations of characters in and around the gospel story. In the 1960s, Martin Bell wrote *The Way of the Wolf*, a collection of short stories, one of which purports to tell why the nine lepers in Luke 17 did not return to Jesus to give thanks. In 1997, *The Red Tent* by Anita Diamant explored the lives of the patriarch Jacob's household. All of these and multitudes more are modern, basically secular examples of the ancient Jewish speculation that is the richness of midrash.

But its richness has not found a firm place in current preaching, teaching, and reflection in the church. It is in that specific interest that the idea of "biblical fracking" is offered. The term is not without its difficult implications. Technically *fracking* is a method of extracting oil and gas from the cracks and crevasses of deep rock formations by applying pressurized liquid to fracture the rock; hence "hydraulic fracking." Its proponents extol access to hitherto unavailable natural resources. Its detractors are concerned about destabilizing the rock formations and possibly polluting the water table. There are similar dangers and advantages in biblical fracking.

Biblical fracking, in the spirit of its historical roots and its geological namesake, means reaching into the cracks and crevasses of the biblical narrative to extract the richness that lurks there. In the spirit of midrash, it wanders and wonders about things that have no authoritative answer. For example, the synoptic gospels tell the story of Jesus teaching in a house in Capernaum when people brought a paralytic on a stretcher to be healed (Luke 5). The press of the crowd was such that they went to the roof, tore back its covering, and lowered the man to Jesus, who subsequently forgave and healed him. It is a wonderful and dramatic story. Fracking the story begins with remembering that Jesus was an itinerant preacher who once famously said that he had no place to lay his head (Matthew 8). So whose house was he in at Capernaum? Whoever it was had agreed to let Jesus use it as a venue for teaching. Knowing his popularity, he may have figured someone would step on his wife's begonias or lean against the rickety fence, but the roof? The text says there was a hue and cry over Jesus presuming to forgive sins. Fracking suggests that in that hubbub the homeowner was looking at the hole in his roof and knowing that he had just given away more than he intended. Seeing him there, eyeing the damage his generosity visited upon him, reminds us of everyone who ever volunteered to do one thing and then found out it was actually several things—serve as treasurer, head the committee, take over the PTA, run a Cub Scout den, or chaperone the field trip. What can one do? What should one do? What is one most likely to do? Exploring those questions in our own lives is the rich return of biblical fracking.

Such speculation is not simply an opportunity to be at play in the fields of the Lord, idly tossing out scriptural fantasies like daydreams or the interpretation of cloud shapes. Fracking can enrich the Christian life in the same way midrash enriches Judaism. In order to do so, it is important that fracking lead us into faith-based reflection on the human experience. To picture our frustrated friend contemplating the assault on his roof without seeing him as an everyman who somehow became more generous than he intended is to miss the potential of fracking. The rich resources of this kind of inquiry can feed the disciplines of preaching and teaching, as well as meditation.

It is important to mark a distinction between midrash and fracking. While those traditions share a common heritage, and fracking is certainly derived from midrash, they are separate. Midrash is Jewish, and fracking is Christian. Each has an interpretive slant, a hermeneutic, that has been shaped by its unique experiences and deepened by its own scholars. In other words, there is an integrity to Judaism and to Christianity that allows them to enrich one another without becoming one. In the same way that a Christian pilgrimage is not a Muslim Haj, nor is a conference center a Hindu ashram, fracking is not midrash.

Fracking can serve as an antidote to excessive biblical piety. The characters and situations that populate the Bible's narratives have rightly been held in high esteem for centuries. We approach them with devotion and expectation. The cumulative effect of this long reverence is that the well-known players have slipped beyond human recognition and identity. Noah is a cartoon; King David is as unreal as Alexander the Great; the disciples are off the charts in the categories of devotion and obtuseness; like a Confederate general, Saint Paul inspires either blind derision or equally blind devotion. We have seen them so much that we rarely see them at all anymore. By fracking their stories, casting our eyes on the scenes and players around them, a new vitality can enter our reflections. What can we learn from Noah's sons (who might have been helped by Adult Children of Alcoholics meetings), or David's General Abner (who carried out his dirty work), or Peter's wife, or Paul's sister? All of them are on the biblical stage, even if they are not at its center. Seeing them and allowing imagination to explore their stories can invigorate stale piety and deepen lively devotion.

The rewards of biblical fracking can be great. But the dangers are also substantial. Imaginative reason operating beyond the reach of Scripture and uninformed by tradition is an invitation to every manifestation of folly to say nothing of sin. Pious human beings have come to incredibly self-serving conclusions with the plain texts of Scripture, proving over and over that the Bible, like a person, can be tortured into saying almost anything. The human tendency to use Scripture to justify bad behavior is multiplied when the plain texts are left behind. Biblical frackers need to be deeply rooted and reliant upon the narratives and mythologies of our faith as the best of our traditions have understood them. Though hardly uniform, the basics of orthodoxy manage to make possible the basic impact of religion, which is to "re-ligament," or put back together, the disparate experiences of life and the ideas of individuals. The treasures yielded by biblical fracking need to be in solid touch, "ligamented" if you will, with Scripture, tradition, and reason. Orthodoxy is the fracker's tether, giving us a faith that is not just personal, but is rooted in the wisdom of the past and the conversations of the present. Without it, there is grave danger of spinning out the Gospel According to Me or, what is worse, the arrogant temptation to be (in my case) the Word becoming Frank and dwelling among you.

Another danger is the pious tendency to make the biblical characters so superhuman that the natural discourses and deductions of life are rendered moot. It is tempting to see biblical scenes the way renaissance artists apparently did, with people falling all over one another in paroxysms of passionate joy, wonder, or fear. I would suggest that life is generally not experienced that way, and since people almost always return to normalcy right after a miracle of one kind or another, we may be safe in toning down our interpretation of those events. The biblical experience was of the supernatural, but it always took place in the natural course of human life. Both mystery and practicality must be kept in mind when exploring Scripture.

The biblical narrative seems to suggest that miracles are not so much mind-blowing suspensions of nature as more subtle events in which some people have perceived God at work. The Exodus provides a case in point. That event was observed by two groups of people, Israelites and Egyptians. The Hebrews and their Christian descendants are still talking about it. The Egyptians have not yet deemed it worthy of comment. The event itself was apparently subtle enough to allow various interpretations. For one it was a miracle of faith-changing dimensions. For the other it was just a bad day at the office.

The continuing wonder at the center of our faith story is that God not only cares about the world but reaches into it in ways that matter. God's reaching in through law, prophets, incarnation, apostles, and the Holy Spirit is the basis for perpetual wonder and praise. But the world into which God reaches is the regular one we all know from experience. Biblical frackers who lace their accounts with the idea that people were so stunned or loved, awed or compelled that the human enterprise was somehow stopped in its tracks have missed the point. The Syro-Phoenician woman (Mark 7) at the well was impressed but not overwhelmed by Jesus. When Jethro, Moses' father-in-law, provided counsel during the Exodus, he was not saving the world, but guiding his inexperienced son-in-law through a management problem (Exod 18). If we separate Bible stories from what we know of the routines of human life, we have no way for those stories to inform and enrich the routines of our lives. Good fracking needs to be consistent with common human experience.

Orthodoxy helps biblical frackers avoid getting lost in their own world. A clear-eyed view of the Bible's stories along with a realistic understanding of human nature can help to avoid over-dramatizing and under-humanizing what we find there.

Armed with an interest in fracking's potential and alert to its dangers, one might wonder how the task is done. There is, of course, no definitive answer. Basic ingredients include speculation and imagination. Notice that both concepts are understood in terms of the absence of defining character. Speculation is developing an idea without a firm foundation. Imagination is developing an idea without reliance on the senses. Speculation and imagination give fracking a free-form element that is not appealing to everyone and may even prove upsetting to some. For others, it can open doors to insight, freshen ancient stories, and initiate dialogue with the Holy Spirit that would otherwise be impossible. It is a tool in the hands of the faithful, a weapon in the hands of the foolish. Fracking a story takes one beyond traditional underpinnings and outside the normal expectations of piety. In addition, fracking wants to lead us to the portals of meditation on faith and life. Good fracking will always raise questions worthy of contemplation and will rarely presume to answer those questions for the reader. Fracking most often begins conversations and seldom brings them to conclusion. These guardrails keep biblical frackers from playing with Scripture and diminishing its challenging and illuminating role in the life of faith.

Different people pursue speculation and unfetter their imagination in different ways. The following considerations, however, might be helpful. Begin with stories. The book of Acts, the gospels, and the history books of the Hebrew Scriptures are generally more fruitful than the theologies of the epistles and the warnings of the prophets. The parables are fair game, along with narrative accounts. The Prodigal Son and family are rich with possibilities, as is the Good Samaritan (what did his wife think of how he spent his time and money?). Picture the story as it unfolds. What is its dramatic center? Begin to look beyond that center to the edges of the story, the people in the shadows. Consider the story from their perspective. What would Palm Sunday look like to a person on the street holding a child's hand? How did Judas Iscariot's mother take the news of his death? How did the Corinthians feel as they read Paul's first letter? Walk around the picture you have made, enter into it and begin to ask questions of it. Scrolling through the five senses can be helpful. What did it look like? What sounds were there? Were there odors? How did the garments, the animals, the walls, or the dust feel against one's skin? What did Cana's wine or the wilderness manna taste like? Let imagination take on the equipment of a movie set as you pan over the crowd, then focus on one person or aspect: the stride of a centurion; the eyes of a Pharisee; the look on the faces of Israelites as they watched Egyptians approach and the waters recede; Zebedee as he watched his sons walk off with Jesus. How would people as I know them respond to that drama? The responses you find can lead to the fruits of biblical fracking.

What follows is an introduction to a plenteous harvest for the faithful mind. It is organized to encourage random reading and intended to extend the reach of traditional Bible study, not mock or distort it. It is meant to connect to the common human experience. It is, hopefully, another way to meet the Lord and be touched by the Spirit through Scripture.

PART ONE

Living in Families

1

Abraham and Sarah

Genesis 22

THOSE WHO HAVE, OR feel they have, a direct line of communication with God are seldom known for their collaborative skills. The patriarchs and prophets of the Old Testament were basically loners. Moses took advice from his father-in-law, but no one else. The gospel stories of Jesus' ministry feature far more give than take. And while Saint Paul seemed to be in constant dialogue with others, the only time he actually changed his mind was on the road to Damascus. Apart from the historical books, the biblical writers were not really interested in what preceded the words and actions they described, but the record we have is where we have to start. And that record describes a long string of unilateral actions informed only by private revelation.

Consider the famous story of the aborted sacrifice of Isaac, one of the great dramatic tales of ancient literature, as well as a foundational story in Judaism, Christianity, and Islam. It is about faithful obedience in the face of terrible consequences. As rich as the story is in drama and meaning, biblical fracking allows us the possibility of finding even more to discover and consider, such as the relationship between Abraham and Sarah, and how it may have played out before the father-son journey to the place of sacrifice.

It would be irresponsible to view the couple through the lens of the modern American family. They were people of their own era living with the mores of that far-off time. We can, however, view them through the lens of our common humanity. Customs, proprieties, and expectations change, but our basic human nature remains fairly constant.

As a family, there was no question as to who made the decisions. Abraham had a direct and exclusive line of communication with God, the kind that renders moot the idea of discussion with others. He also had the cultural authority to offer his wife to Pharaoh's harem and Abimelech's roving eye in order to protect himself from danger. But Sarah was not without resources. She was able to persuade her husband, against his wishes, to exile Hagar and Ishmael in order to protect her son Isaac from familial competition. Obviously, there was give and take in the relationship, even if the particulars seem strange to us.

So, what happened to Sarah's protective instincts and persuasive powers as Abraham inched toward the awful decision to offer their only son as a sacrifice? Did Abraham tell her what he was going to do? Probably not, because with God's word and his own familial authority there was no need, and he would have been loath to unleash Sarah's well-known protective instincts and persuasive powers. But the decision must have weighed heavily on his heart and mind to such a degree that Sarah would have known something was wrong.

Look into Sarah's heart, where she can sense the absence of candor in her husband, where she struggles to learn from words not spoken, and tries to interpret an unknown. Demons of fear and suspicion thrive in such a climate, and make learning and interpreting even more difficult. She may have told herself that it was nothing to worry about, but the dark spirits of suspicion would not buy it. Could she ask him? Maybe. Maybe not. Let us assume that, since the Scriptures do not include her role in this awful scene, she chose to be as silent as her husband and, like him, kept the drama inside.

Look into Abraham's heart, where there is a terrible clarity sitting across his path like a snarling beast. He is caught in a classic moral dilemma: the conflict of equally compelling virtues. His love for God and his love for his son are on a collision course. One must be obeyed and the other discounted. To turn away from God would be to make a lie of everything he has ever said or done. He is Abraham, whose obedience to God defines not only his life but the entire enterprise of faith and belief. On the other hand, Isaac is his only son—the son of God's promise, the means by which his name and his faith would be carried to future generations. The fact that he chose God over Isaac could not have removed the clouds of doubt and pain from his heart or his countenance.

With his terrible decision made, Abraham must concentrate on it the way a marksman focuses on a target or a surgeon eyes an artery. The other horn of his dilemma, the love for Isaac, can easily hook him and pull him away from his chosen path. There is no place for distractions, as Sarah certainly would be if he told her. His wife could have made the choice between God and Isaac in a heartbeat, and it would not have conformed to that of her husband. So Abraham is silent, left alone to face the beast. And Sarah is left to the demons of fear and suspicion. Each suffers acutely but differently. That is what happens when people who share a life do not share life's burdens.

The story resolves itself along the lines of the adage "I faced some terrible things in my life and most of them never happened." While that is often true and ends the drama in this case, it is not always so; sometimes the demons of fear and suspicion are allowed to play havoc with our tranquility.

How did Abraham and Sarah deal with their solitary burdens? There is, of course, no record. But we can be sure that they, like the rest of us, had to address, live with, or flee from their experience. How might their individual burdens have been lightened if they had talked to one another? Could their powerful, but solitary, experiences have a corrosive effect on their marriage? Talking requires courage and trust. Silence, when there is much to say, corrupts and tarnishes.

2

David and Abner

2 Samuel 3

SOME FOUR HUNDRED YEARS before the birth of Christ, Athens and Sparta clashed in what is called the Peloponnesian War. In the course of that conflict, mighty Athens overran the small island of Melos. As Thucydides recorded, the Athenian rationale was "the strong do what they can and the weak suffer what they must." It would be difficult to imagine a better motto for the world's bullies. Humanity has never wanted for seemingly strong men and women who prey on the seemingly weak. Neither the Bible nor our own day is lacking in examples. It is possible that fracking a scriptural account of bullies at work may lead to, if not open, a window of insight into their world.

Consider the story of powerful King David and Army Commander Abner along with three unfortunates: King Saul's son and daughter, Ishbaal and Michal, and Michal's husband Paltiel. The background is the up-and-down relationship between David and Israel's first king, Saul. During an up period, Saul wed his daughter Michal to young David. During a downturn, he took her back and gave her to Paltiel. After Saul's death, David fought to establish himself as the rightful king and came into conflict with the forces of Saul's son Ishbaal led by Abner, a man who would fit anyone's idea of a bully. In the confusion of disorderly succession in the House of Saul, Ishbaal was concerned that Abner was getting too close to one of Saul's concubines. This was not just a matter of romantic dalliance, but Abner's assertion of rights to the king's property and ultimately the king's throne. Abner responded to Ishbaal's accusation with the kind of self-righteous indignation that bullies resort to when guilty. Abner's rant succeeded in intimidating Ishbaal so that he "could not answer Abner another word, because he feared him." Capitulation like that feeds the bully's contempt for the victim and often inflates the image of himself as invincible. Perhaps because of his disdain for Ishbaal or because of his guilt, Abner switched sides. David, sensing the upper hand Abner's betrayal gave him, and wanting to assert his own claim to Saul's throne, demanded that Ishbaal strip Michal from Paltiel and let Abner bring her back. Ishbaal did as he was told. Paltiel joined the ranks of victims by following Michal and Abner down the road "weeping as he walked behind her." This continued until Abner, ever the bully, snarled "Go back home," and Paltiel did so.

While it is true that laying claim to King Saul's concubine and his daughter were political moves, the behavior of David and Abner provides insight into the particular kind of blindness manifested in bullies throughout the ages. Did they see what they were doing to Ishbaal and Paltiel? Did anyone give a thought to Michal as she was bounced from husband to husband? Fracking the story suggests that they did not. Abner could see the physical shapes of his victims, but not their humanity or their claim on dignity. As with cyber bullies today, David's blindness was deepened by the fact that he could not see the effect his demands had on his victims. It is unlikely that David and Abner had any perception of themselves as overinflated egotists relying on the weak to make themselves appear strong.

The blindness of bullies comes in part from the glare of their own needs, which prevents them from seeing the rights, privileges, and needs of others. The overwhelming neediness of a bully might be political or psychological, sexual or social, economic or egotistical, but it prevents the oppressor from seeing—literally taking into account—the people he is pushing around. When the response of those victims reinforces the bully's distorted self-image, the blindness is deepened to near-total darkness. That may provide an insight but in no way an excuse for the behavior. As the saying goes, "there are none so blind as those who will not see."

In the time of Saul and David, and well beyond, few people actually saw women in their fullness as human beings. They were bartering chips, commodities, and baby-makers. I doubt that David could see all of Michal's humanity. Ishbaal joined the bullies in their blindness and became an enabler by letting fear block every alternative except serving as their tool. Paltiel's weeping dissent and easy acquiescence complimented the blindness by feeding Abner's tough-guy picture of himself. It takes courage to live in the world as it really is with people who are fully human. Bullies universally lack that courage and cover their deficit with blind aggression. Frightened enablers like Ishbaal and satisfying victims like Paltiel play their part. As Jesus once said (Matt 15:14), when the blind lead the blind, both fall into the ditch.

3

Zebedee

Mark 1:16–20

WEALTH IS MORALLY AND spiritually complicated. The arrogance and excesses of those who succumb to its temptations have long been a source of pain in the world. The prophet Amos derided the insensitivity of the rich (6:4–7), and Jesus commented on how hard it is for them to enter God's kingdom (Mark 10:25). Many of the world's revolutions, both great and small, have been rooted in frustration with their indulgences; the unequal distribution of wealth continues to vex communities and nations. Even when wealth's power accomplishes great things, as it often does, there is the subtle temptation for the donor to believe that since he is doing God a favor, it will be returned. Does not scripture (Eccl 11:1) tell us to "send out your bread upon the waters, after many days you will get it back"? A sense of entitlement with a dash of elitism naturally follows such a line of thought. In spite and perhaps because of its obvious benefits, wealth creates a moral and spiritual landscape that is difficult to navigate.

The story of Zebedee, the father of the disciples James and John, draws us into that difficult terrain. The texts suggest that he was a man of means, while the story unfolding around him hints at how he might have borne the mantle of wealth. Fracking his

story raises questions without answering them, suggests possibilities without proving them, and invites us to glimpse our own story
in his.

Zebedee is only identified directly when Jesus calls his sons
to follow him. Mark tells us they were mending fishing nets when
Jesus pulled the two young men away, leaving Zebedee behind
with the hired men. Luke indicates that Zebedee and his sons were
partners with Simon Peter in a fishing enterprise (5:10). Some
key assumptions can be drawn from those few details. One is that
Zebedee had a boat in a business that was successful enough for
him to employ others. Secondly, his sons and his business partner
all joined the Jesus Movement and left him behind. Matthew adds
another layer to that image by recording that Zebedee's wife was
also part of Jesus' entourage. She asked him to promise that her
sons would have high positions in the kingdom Jesus proclaimed,
proving that helicopter parents existed long before helicopters and
that she did not quite grasp the meaning of Jesus' message. She
was, however, present at the crucifixion (Matt 27:56) and perhaps
the resurrection (Luke 23:55—24:12), which indicates the depth
of her involvement. For our purposes, it further isolates Zebedee
back home by the lake as his wife, sons, and business associate all
fell in behind the charismatic Nazarene.

We have no access to his thoughts or feelings except what we
may infer from our common humanity. Frustration and resentment are easy to assume. Why wouldn't one feel that way if one's
family and partner took off for what could easily be a lark at best or
a scam at worst? What feelings naturally emerge in those who remain in the routine while others go forth to newness? How could
the mundane task of mending nets compare to whatever Jesus
meant by fishing for people? Such sentiments may be natural, but
they are based on a degree of helplessness in the face of circumstance. Yet Zebedee was anything but helpless. In this patriarchal
society, he was a patriarch. The details of his agreement with Peter
may have limited his options in that regard, but there were no
limits to his authority over his wife and sons. He could, of course,
have been a milquetoast who would not stand up to his family.

But running a successful fishing business on the Sea of Galilee was not a role for the fainthearted, nor was the mercurial Simon Peter likely to be the easiest of partners. If Zebedee stayed behind while everyone else, left he probably had a good reason to do so.

His reasons cannot be known, but it is reasonable to think that Zebedee might have shared the enthusiasm of his family and could not join in their journey for physical or even fiscal reasons. Itinerant preaching and teaching required a form of stamina distinct from the demands of a fishing business. It is also possible that Zebedee needed to maintain the financial base on which the itinerants depended. While Scripture tells us that Jesus and the disciples all had professions, there are no accounts of them actually practicing their trades while travelling. John tells us that Judas "kept the common purse" for the group. Where might the coins for that purse come from? Undoubtedly there were many generous supporters of Jesus' ministry. Could Zebedee, whose family and partner were so heavily invested in Jesus' ministry, have been a major donor? If he were, would it not have been a deeply satisfying investment? Jesus's miraculous acts of healing and his fresh teaching were the talk of Galilee (Luke 4:14), which would have allowed Zebedee to bask in reflected glory. How sweet it is when doing the right thing turns out to be a good thing. It is sweeter still when that good thing is publicly applauded, as countless plaques, building names, and statues attest.

Our story could end here with a good feeling all around. Except that wealth, even when it is applied generously, remains part of a challenging moral and spiritual landscape. Zebedee's story continues beyond the resurrection.

The small Jerusalem church, with the Zebedee sons prominent in its ranks, experienced the power of Pentecost, organizing itself for care of its own and for evangelism in the community. As the church's popularity on the street grew, so did opposition from the temple, fanned by the disturbing rumor that the followers of Jesus were reaching out to gentiles. Leaders were regularly harassed by officials, culminating in the stoning of a deacon named Stephen (Acts 6:8—7:60). Luke tells us that King Herod soon joined in the persecution and had "James the brother of John killed with the sword" (Acts 12:2). In time, word of his son's death would have reached Zebedee and driven him into the moral and spiritual wilderness of Gold Star parents in every generation and culture. The death of a child, even an adult child in a worthy cause, is a cruel violation of human expectation. They are supposed to mourn us, not we them. How could this be the result of such high hopes, lofty principles, and generous love? Wouldn't it be better to be mending nets in Galilee than lying in honor in Jerusalem? Was this to be the return on his investment? In a darker vein, was Zebedee somehow the cause of his son's death? If he had not encouraged him, would he still be alive? Or worse, was it his meddling wife's fault, a question that would tear at the fabric of what was left of his family? Is that what the power of his wealth brought into being?

Did Zebedee regain perspective? Could he place his pain alongside his offerings of money and influence? Did he realize that doing what is right is still right even when it hurts? The cool reasoning that is possible from our objective historical perch was not available to him. Grief has a way of narrowing one's field of vision, and with it the ability to set loss in the larger contexts of hope, purpose, and possibility. That happens to all who grieve. But those who must mourn the painful outcome of their generosity, goodness, and responsible stewardship have a particularly stony path to follow. It is difficult terrain.

4

Households

Matthew 8:14–15; Luke 2:41–52; John 2:1–11

WHEN JESUS RETURNED TO Nazareth, we are told that the Lord's familiarity in the community prevented any "deeds of power" and led him to opine, "Prophets are not without honor except in their own country and in their own house" (Matt 13:57). Many centuries later, editor and critic Eric Larrabee suggested, "The prophet is without honor in his own country precisely because his own countrymen have to listen to him all the time." While we might regret Larrabee's apparent lack for respect for prophetic figures, we can appreciate his insight into their families. The biblical spotlight is obviously and properly focused on the major players in Scripture with little interest in those who share day to day life with them. Few contemporary readers realize that Moses had a wife and children, Jesus had siblings, Peter had a wife, and Paul a sister. Fracking allows us to consider those relationships and in doing so shed some light on our own families.

Consider the experience of Zipporah, the wife of Moses. We meet her in the aftermath of Moses' impetuous murder of an Egyptian overseer who was harshly treating a Hebrew worker. The future law-giver fled into the wilderness where, in classic folklore form, he gallantly came to the defense of young ladies, was invited home to supper, and ended up married. Trying to peer into a time so far from our own provides only the dimmest hints about the couple and their relationship. Zipporah means "bird," which gives a wholly unwarranted but intriguing suggestion as to her size and demeanor. Marriages at this time were practical affairs representing the relationships between patriarchs more than between lovers It is possible to imagine that Zipporah would have been regarded by these ancient men much like modern men regard pickup trucks: can she do the job without undue offense to the eye?

Such a bargain was to be expected in Zipporah's world. Her feelings may or may not have been considered, but it is most unlikely that she had none. It is not, however, unreasonable to guess that Zipporah was satisfied. After her initial encounter with Moses, she described him to her father as "an Egyptian" (Exod 2:19), a sophisticated status in the eyes of flock-tending nomads. And she was able to do the tasks expected of a wife in those days. She gave birth to two sons, Gershom and Eliezer (the latter not to be confused with Abraham's servant). The family settled into what we may assume was a contented routine of well-being, with Moses tending his father-in-law Jethro's flocks.

But the hand of God does not always respect the bounds or the bonds of domestic tranquility. It tapped Moses on the shoulder. The same hand that pushed him toward the cruel overseer set fire to a bush and would not let it go out. After much hemming and hawing, Moses set out to confront Pharaoh and lead God's chosen people to freedom. Before doing so, however, he gave Zipporah and the two boys back to her father. On the obviously positive side, Moses' task would be hard enough without adding a wife and children to the mix. On the obviously painful side, nobody likes the sense of inadequacy and failure that comes with being sent home.

After the great drama that history knows as the Exodus, Moses returned with his newly freed rabble to Jethro's mountain, the one we call Sinai. Exodus 18 gives us a poignant scene when viewed from the perspective of families. Jethro came to meet

Moses and brought along Zipporah and the boys. We are told that the two men bowed and kissed one another and then went into the tent. Did Moses and Bird exchange a glance, a touch of the hand? Did the great man rough the hair of his son's heads as fathers have done forever? Was there a word, full of meaning or even full of awkwardness? We have no way of knowing. The silence of the text gives us only a picture of Zipporah and her sons outside a tent where their past was being weighed and their future determined. The lack of any further mention of the mother and sons strongly suggests that they remained with Jethro while Moses headed for glory.

It seems like an odd decision for Moses to make. The Chosen People had many families among them. Zipporah, Gershom, and Eliezer would not have been any form of an anomaly in such a setting. It is also odd that Moses let go of the very thing to which Abraham clung so desperately—progeny. In the understanding of this age, children and grandchildren were the only way a man's life continued beyond death. Was Moses so singular in his preoccupation with leading God's people that these considerations were set aside? We must assume so.

But Moses could not have been so focused that there was not a moment of recognition of the finality of this phase of his life. And Bird could not have been so much like a pickup truck that she did not at least wince at the parting. Even if she was glad to see Moses go, parting always has an element of "sweet sorrow." Do we not take a final walk through the house before the moving van pulls out? Doesn't even a necessary divorce leave some shiny pieces behind? Don't we secretly pause over the old stains on a well-worn shirt before we place it in the rag bag? Do we not savor the last cookie before a diet begins? Endings, even when they stand so close to beginnings, claim their own emotional territory in relationships. No matter what duties and devotions sent Moses and Zipporah in opposite directions, it must have been a moment that every human heart can feel.

Applying the principles of fracking to the Holy Family must give pause to even a blithe spirit, but it can be done, especially since our current focus is on Jesus' siblings. What must it have been like to have Jesus as a big brother? He was a child of precocious abilities, if the story of his interactions with the temple teachers is to be credited. Many of us know what it is to follow in the footsteps of a wunderkind—all of the teachers expect you to be as good or better. It is a well-known childhood burden.

Another possible glimpse into the Holy Household can be seen through the story of the wedding at Cana, where Jesus turned water into wine. When the wine at the celebration ran out, Mary reported the problem to Jesus. Perhaps sensing that he was being set up, Jesus said, "Woman what concern is that to you and me? My hour has not yet come." Ignoring his plea, Mary told the servants to do whatever Jesus said. The result is one of Jesus' first *public* miracles. The emphasis is on public because a little fracking clearly suggests that there were some *private* miracles beforehand. How else would Mary have known that Jesus could do anything about the wine problem? Perhaps Jesus had been taking care of the adult beverage needs of the family for years. Mark indicates that there were other private miracles. His rendering of the story of Jesus walking on the water includes the significant fact that "He intended to pass them by" (Mark 6:48), meaning he had no intention of impressing the disciples with his command of nature, but simply wanted to use the shortest route to Bethsaida. If this is so, is it impious to think that the feeding miracles might have been lab-tested in Mary's kitchen? Did Jesus quietly heal his siblings of the common maladies that afflicted other Nazarene children?

What would it have been like to grow up with such a brother? His star quality would have been a boon to the family, but most likely a burden to his siblings, whose concerns did not extend to the source of things they enjoyed. Children are tiny eddies of self-interest asking only how people and events effect their immediate well-being. Was Jesus sensitive to that reality? There is no way to tell except to note that, as an adult, Jesus was wise, insightful, compassionate, focused, and powerful. I would not add "sensitive" to the list.

If it is true, as some suggest, that Joseph died shortly after the temple story, Jesus would have become something like the head of the household in that male-dominated culture. Younger brothers and sisters, testing the limits of their freedoms, as children must, probably experienced Jesus as they do all authority figures—insufferable. If, as others have suggested, the siblings were Joseph's by a previous marriage, then Jesus would have been the youngest. Since children naturally respect the rank that age confers, being Jesus' big brother would almost be worse than being his little brother. Being outshined by someone you should outrank is particularly galling. Growing up with Jesus would have been hard, even if it did have some fringe benefits like free food and in-house medical care.

The Bible names four brothers of Jesus: James, Joseph, Jude, and Simon. An unknown number of sisters go unnamed. The book of Acts mentions only one of the brothers, James, who provided significant leadership in the Jerusalem congregation. The Gospel writer John tells us that Jesus placed his mother in John's care. What became of Jesus' other siblings? Did they really abandon their mother or stepmother to the care of John Bar Zebedee? (John 19:26). Did they do what people in small towns have always done when a member was condemned as a felon, and just quit talking about him? Were they so scarred by growing up in Jesus' shadow that they could not forget him quickly enough? Or did they, like so many since, find it difficult to believe that he is indeed the Son of God? C. S. Lewis has maintained that Jesus is either the messianic incarnation of God or an impossible madman. Even brothers and sisters have to decide which.

The Bible is essentially a book about God, so developing the stories of those who interact with God is a secondary concern. Of all the humans who appear in the Bible, only a handful emerge as developed characters. The patriarch Jacob comes to mind, as does King David. Jesus is certainly central, but manages to remain personally elusive. Saint Paul can be glimpsed behind his epistles, but none stand out like the impulsive and passionate apostle Simon Peter. His story is writ so large in Scripture and tradition that fracking is not necessary to see him clearly. For our purposes, we can note his predilection for snap judgments followed by adjustments, as when he named Jesus as the Messiah and then disagreed with him about what that meant (Mark 8:27–33). His embarrassing tendency to over-promise and under-perform can be seen in his failed attempt to walk on water (Matt 14:28–31) and the classic assertion that he would stand by Jesus no matter what, only to fold under the scrutiny of a night-shift serving maid (Mark 14:66–72). In telling the story of the transfiguration, Luke and Mark find it necessary to point out that Peter did not know what he was talking about when he blurted the idea that Jesus might be the equal of Moses and Elijah (Luke 9:33; Mark 9:6). Peter is a force of nature, often wrong but seldom in doubt. His heart is dangerously ahead of his thinking; he is passionate, and easier to love than to live with.

Which brings us to what it must have been like to be part of Peter's family. He, of course, had a brother named Andrew who shared his commitment to Jesus. They may also have shared some personal characteristics, as might be suggested in Andrew's assertion that "We have found the Messiah" after a brief visit with Jesus (John 1:41). The more intriguing family dynamic is Peter's marital relationship. Matthew, Mark, and Luke all refer to Jesus healing Peter's mother-in-law. In that day as in this, marriage was the only way to acquire one of those. What would it have been like to be married to such a passionate, impulsive, flawed, and lovable person?

In the first century, women were basically commodities to be exchanged in the interests of male alliances and (preferably male) babies. Feelings were not a prime consideration, but as in the case of Zipporah, we cannot assume they were absent. Genuine affection was more than possible, even if it was not guaranteed.

We obviously can know nothing of Peter's wife. My guess is that her biblical absence suggests she had died by the time Jesus came into Peter's life. Peter's unfettered commitment to the itinerant Jesus implies that the disciple and his wife had no children. The possibility that Peter and his mother-in-law established a beneficial relationship of home (his) and hearth (hers) is not beyond imagining. All of this would have been after the death of Peter's wife.

But what of life before that untimely end? What would it have been like to share a home with such a quixotic spirit? Not dull, whatever else it might have been. Life would have been cluttered with half-finished projects, suddenly invited guests, unbudgeted purchases, and patience-stretching delays. It is possible that Peter was not the only one cut out for sainthood. But along with the challenges, there would have been angelic intent, unabashed love, fervor in all of its forms, and a lot of laughter for those who could enjoy such a life. To be happy with someone like Peter, it is necessary to prefer the collateral damage of passion to the calculated results of precision.

Was Peter's wife constitutionally capable of living such a life? We cannot know. Some are. Most are not. There is no special laurel for those who are drawn to it, and no condemnation for those who are not. Relationships are a matter of chemistry, the result of the combination of two or more personalities. The relationship of Peter and his spouse would have been extreme—extremely exciting or extremely miserable. Which outcome was not determined by either one of them, but by the chemistry between them.

The individuals who stand out in the biblical narrative have personalities writ large. Living with them requires a great deal and may deliver a lot less. Families who willingly or unwillingly find themselves in such an unequal equation have always been with us and provide insight into the people around the great saints. The book of Acts gives us the briefest of hints about Saint Paul's family, but it is enough for us to sketch at least an outline of one of his siblings.

In Acts 23, Paul was in the midst of the predictable turmoil that seemed to attend his every appearance. The Roman authorities in Jerusalem had him in protective custody, but the Jewish authorities were plotting what would later be called a lynching. Acts 23:16 tells us "Now the son of Paul's sister heard about the ambush; so he went and gained entrance to the barracks and told Paul." The plot twists are fascinating, but fracking takes us off that well-worn path to consider what it must have been like to be Paul's sister. She is, of course, unnamed in the text, but since we are seeking her as a person, it helps to have a name for her. I am choosing Rebecca.

Fortunately Paul's writings tell us a good bit about his family, including Rebecca. They were from Tarsus, a political capital and major trading center located on what is now Turkey's Mediterranean coast. Their parents were Roman citizens, which established them in the social if not necessarily the financial elite. They were devout Jews, still aware of their tribal genealogy (Benjamin) long after those distinctions defined Hebrew culture. Their theological and political identity was as Pharisees, the strictest brand of Judaism then current. They had the ambition and the means to send their son off to the equivalent of the Ivy League, Gamaliel's "school" in Jerusalem. No such educational opportunity was available for Rebecca, of course, but as a Roman citizen, she enjoyed privileges beyond the reach of most women, including the ownership of property, engaging in business, and, in certain circumstances, obtaining a divorce.

Paul and Rebecca grew up in the express lanes of life, unlikely to be troubled by whatever it was that impeded the common traffic. That they (or at least Paul) acquired a somewhat haughty air is suggested in this exchange with a Roman tribune. "The tribune came and asked Paul, "Tell me, are you a Roman citizen?" And he said "Yes." The tribune answered, "It cost me a large sum of money to get my citizenship." Paul said, "But I was born a citizen" (Acts 22:27–28). It does not require excessive fracking to hear the imperious tone that club members use when speaking to someone eager but unqualified to join. Since we have no words of Rebecca's, we cannot be sure she had a similar attitude. We can, however, assume that she continued to live in the express lane after her move to Jerusalem. Her son had the confidence and the credentials to gain entrance to the Roman barracks and an audience with the tribune, not a path readily open to commoners.

While all we can make is a sketch of Paul's family, it is possible to see signs of a comfortable, successful, well-established, and pious household. That Rebecca and her parents took great pride in the overachieving young Pharisee is more than likely—which would have made his conversion to a strange sect that was "everywhere . . . spoken against" (Acts 28:22) especially painful.

Family speculation in such circumstances usually begins with the newly blackened sheep. "How *could* he? He had every advantage? Perhaps he is ill." This phase is usually brief and quickly turns to blame. "He must have fallen in with a bad crowd!" "Where did we go wrong?" "Nobody on *my* side of the family ever did anything like this!" "It was the liberal education of Gamaliel that did it!" This line of conversation can run for a long time, but it is soon joined by more basic and personal concerns. "I am so embarrassed!" "How can I hold my head up any longer?" "That busybody Lucretia will have a field day with this!" "My political career is over." "No respectable person will want to marry Rebecca after this gets out."

The conversion of Saint Paul is a feast day in the church (January 25) and the subject of great artists like Caravaggio, as well as many others. It marks a turning point in the Christian story as our faith found its first theologian and a key to the double-locked door that had long excluded gentiles from the fruits of Judaism. It is a defining moment for the church. And it was a defining moment for a comfortable, successful, well-established and pious household in Tarsus. Could they have wondered about the real source and meaning of their pain? Did they love Paul because of the pride they enjoyed through him? If that is true to any extent, is that loving Paul or loving what they get by loving Paul? Were they able to separate what they thought and felt about Paul from the way others regarded him? Did Paul, who persuaded whole communities of Christ's divinity, have any luck explaining it to his family?

There is no evidence that they joined him in his attraction to the Christian sect. But did they at least understand him as a human being, if not as an evangelist? There is a wisp of evidence about that. It seems that Rebecca was still there after all of her brother's troubles and their impact on the family. Paul and the tribune both refer to Rebecca's son as a "young man." Can we assume that he was too young to be hanging out at the Roman barracks without his parent's permission? If so, Rebecca was still there, behind the scenes, with or without understanding or even appreciation of her brother's behavior. If so, she bears witness to a family bond that can absorb blows to its comfort, success, standing, and even beliefs without breaking. If so, Rebecca at least loved Paul more than what loving Paul gave her.

5

The Saints of Joppa

Acts 9:36–42; Ephesians 6 1–20

THERE ARE MANY PROFOUNDLY spiritual moments in life. Some—like retreats, pilgrimages and devotional disciplines—are sought out. Others are surprises, like holding one's firstborn, seeing the stars without city light, or finding undeserved forgiveness. Among them all, the death of a loved one seems to lay unique spiritual claims on believers and nonbelievers alike. Relationships seem to have a nonstop feature that allows us to live in them without contemplating an end, even though we know there will be one. We can anticipate our own death with wills, wishes, and powers of attorney, but it seems morbid to do the same for loved ones. It is also true that the fact of death is so different from any contemplation of it that there is always a shock, even when its approach is obvious. For these and other reasons, the death of loved ones leaves us unanchored and vulnerable when spiritual forces begin to swirl around us. Fracking the story of the Saints of Joppa provides a rich opportunity for exploring the intense subtlety of one of the particular tasks of grief: waiting.

The events took place very early in the Christian story (when all believers were referred to as saints). In those days, congregations often included a subgroup of widows, women whose family connections had been lost through death and whose essential community was the church. Tabitha may well have been among them, since only the church seems to be involved. Perhaps because her death was unexpected or because she was such a key player in congregational life, the survivors needed help in dealing with it. So, according to custom, her body was washed and laid in a room upstairs. But counter to custom, the tiny Christian community reached out to Peter instead of the leaders of their Jewish congregation. That decision set up the spiritual struggle that took place in Joppa.

Peter was in Lydda, about ten miles away. At even a quickened pace due to the urgency of the request, it would take three to four hours to get there. It may have taken a while to find Peter and deliver the message, and it probably took Peter some time to prepare for the journey back. If the messengers left Joppa at noon, it would have been close to 6 pm before they were ready to return. There was no real way to travel after sundown, so they would have waited until sunrise to set out, arriving in Joppa around 9 am, twenty-one hours after their departure. Those hours provided the arena for the spiritual struggle.

What would the Saints of Joppa do in that twenty-one-hour period? Tabitha's body had already been prepared. There was no family to notify. They undoubtedly prayed for her and for one another. Perhaps a meal was prepared for the anticipated visitors. Then they waited. And waiting is the Devil's Time, a prime condition for spiritual conflict.

Waiting is a vulnerable time because it is defined by the absence of something. It is different from idleness, which can provide its own reasons for being. Waiting is the no-man's-land between what was and what will be. There is nothing to hold onto. The present has lost touch with both the past and the future, which allows unrealistic assumptions and unreasonable doubts to assert themselves. This would not have happened if I had been more attentive—as if life and death were ours to control. Nothing is worth doing now—as if Tabitha held the single key to meaningful life. My faith is weak or perhaps even useless, since it neither prevents misfortune nor assuages pain—as if that were the reason for believing. When Jesus' friend Lazarus died, his sister Mary spoke from the confused turmoil of waiting when she confronted Jesus: "If you had been here my brother would not have died" (John 11:32)—as if there were a secret agreement to spare her family from life's only certainty. Such thoughts are common at a time of death. They seem to make sense in the darkness of the "valley of the shadow of death" where the light of reason is dimmed.

The Saints of Joppa may or may not have had the insight to know they were being buffeted by absurd notions and groundless doubts. Hopefully they were close enough and trusted one another enough to say what they were thinking, because many assumptions and doubts turn to mist when put into words. But the messengers and Peter did not return until the next morning, which means that each of the saints went to bed where, before sleep, the demons of doubt and distortion roam freely with no one to call them by their right names.

The forces of evil within and around us are easily identified in those twenty-one hours. But what was God doing while they waited for Peter and the demons had their day? Did the Lord provide glimmers of hope? If so, it was for the next life, not this one. Any assumptions they had about what was coming certainly did not include Tabitha being returned to life, as actually happened. What could they count on while sitting in that no-man's-land between that which was no longer and that which is not yet?

Paul's letter to the Ephesians probably had not been written in time to benefit the Saints of Joppa, but its wisdom can help us to see what God might have been doing in those long hours. In the sixth chapter of that letter, Paul urges his readers to be strong in the Lord by putting on "the whole armor of God." Paul's words are stirring and worthy of meditation at any time. In the waiting hours of grief, however, the ultimate reason for donning God's armor is especially significant. It is so that "on that evil day [we will] stand firm." The point is not progress, but steadiness. God does not come to us to fix the perils of waiting, to banish the darkness of death with unreal light. Healing, forgiveness, reconciliation, and renewal all have their day, but for now the answer remains "not yet." Faith does not protect us from dismay, doubt, and distortion; rather, faith equips us to stand firm in their midst. That is what God offered in Joppa and continues to offer today.

If that seems like a cold, unsatisfying bargain, consider the insights of C. S. Lewis in *The Screwtape Letters*, the fanciful account of a senior demon, Screwtape, advising his young nephew, Wormwood, how to carry out spiritual warfare on Satan's behalf. Screwtape describes the motives of God during periods like those in Joppa: "He leaves the creature to stand up on its own legs—to carry out from the will alone duties that have lost all relish. It is during the trough periods, much more than the peak periods, that it is growing into the sort of creature He wants it to be . . . Our cause is never more in danger than when a human, no longer desiring, but still intending, to do our Enemy's will, looks upon a universe from which every trace of Him seems to have vanished, and asks why he has been forsaken, and still obeys."[1]

What did Peter find when he arrived in Joppa and provided an end to the long wait? There is no way to know, but one can hope he found a community at least somewhat encased in God's armor, and just a little more like the sort of creatures God wants them to be.

---

1. C. S. Lewis, *The Screwtape Letters with Screwtape Proposes a Toast* (New York: HarperCollins, 2014), 40.

6

Noah and His Sons

Genesis 9:18–29

THE STORY OF NOAH is well-established in both our faith tradition and our culture. Few children grow up without some exposure to it. Nurseries of believers and nonbelievers alike are festooned with rainbows, overloaded arks, and Noah's happy family. The common story is, however, selective. I do not refer to the obvious omission of a catastrophic flood and mass drowning, but to the second part of Noah's story, the one that raises questions about substance abuse and its consequences in a family. Familiar storytelling stops short of this troubling sequence, simply because it is troubling. No case can be made for depicting the strange story on children's walls but, for whatever reason, it is part of the biblical narrative and worthy of adult consideration. On the surface, it seems to offer little or nothing for our spiritual appetite, but by fracking the story, possibilities for serious reflection begin to present themselves.

The tale is a simple one. Noah planted a vineyard after the flood and got drunk on its wine—so drunk that he passed out and fell naked in his tent. His son Ham found him and in so doing apparently committed a grave sin. The text does not help us to understand the nature of that error. Ham informed his two brothers, who elaborately covered their father by walking backward into the tent and dropping a cloak over him. Noah's outrage when he learned of Ham's offense resulted in what has come to be known as "the curse of Ham,"—perpetual slavery.

Fracking such an obscure story is relatively easy, since there are so many unexplained elements. One can, with cautious respect, identify Noah's alcoholic behavior and its profound affect on his children. In such a setting, the home becomes a shrine to an angry god who demands ritual dishonesty and misplaced guilt.

Alcoholics and other addicts readily blame others for their behavior, and when the addict has power in the way parents do, children are often required to shoulder that blame, creating scars that can last a lifetime. Noah apparently accepted no responsibility for his behavior, but leveled blame squarely on Ham's inadvertent intrusion. Families often develop baroque rituals in order to conform to the alternate reality that the god of addiction imposes. Shem and Japheth walking backward to place a cloak over their father is not unlike other family cover-ups that shield the truth from prying eyes. "Daddy is not feeling well"; "Mother is tired and taking a nap"; "he wanted to come to your game but he was busy"; "someone needs to fix that carpet so others don't trip on it"; and "the brakes must have failed" are all variations on Noah's sons' literal cover-up.

If one can accept that Noah's behavior in these verses corresponds to that of an addict, bending himself and his family into the contorted reality that addiction so often demands, how might that have come to be? How could this blameless man who walked with God become a slave to a tyrannical demi-god like alcohol? Sad history proves that the path to addiction is well-worn by the righteous as well as the unrighteous. One common aspect of such a journey is that it is done slowly. Fracking Noah's story takes us into the silent phase of the narrative, the time that passed between the ark and the addiction. Consider the laxity, the letting-go that often accompanies the completion of a great task, like building and commanding the ark. The demands of concentration, discipline, and control in that situation would have been significant, which means that the release from them must have been equally significant. The lapse that follows great effort is a soft place where the broader sense of responsibility can dim. The need for tending the ark might have passed, but the need for tending the body and soul never cease. Temporal responsibilities come and go, but temptations are constant. That vital distinction is easy to forget when a demanding phase of life is completed.

A boiling rage rose like bile in Noah when he realized that Ham had witnessed the nakedness of his body, compromising his self-image and his moral authority. The side of himself he worked so hard to deny was exposed. The strength of his resolutions was shown to be gauze, his commitment to discipline was melted wax. It was too much to contain and too bitter to swallow, so he spewed it out on the one closest to him, in this case the unfortunate Ham.

Noah's path into addiction's embrace would not have been simple nor would it have relied on rational decisions in favor of excess. Addiction is a complex interplay between chemistry, experience, opportunity, and environment. Modern medicine knows it to be a disease, albeit an opportunistic one involving decisions that create and sustain vulnerability. It is as subtle as the snake in Eden's Garden, beguiling and promising. It is a false god demanding all and returning nothing. It grows in life like a cataract in the eye, unnoticeably clouding vision so that what used to be obvious silently disappears. That can happen to the hopes and even the importance of those we love; it can happen to responsibilities and integrity; to honesty, decency, and life itself, none of which are consciously rejected. One simply loses sight of them, allowing them to be replaced by the false promise that the next step in service to addiction will do what is desired.

As Noah followed this path, his patriarchal authority drew his sons along with him. The father's gradual inability to focus on relationships, responsibilities, and respect imposed a dishonest, uncaring, and unreal world on those who depended on him. In that addiction-dominated world, Ham believed that seeing his father's nakedness was somehow his fault. Shem and Japheth believed that a literal cover-up was what was required. What else could they do? How can children, even adult children, know when a parent is out of control? How can one hold on to self-respect when a powerful figure in his or her life is meting out unwarranted blame?

While the brief eleven-verse story of Noah and his sons is likely to remain obscure to even the most vigorous of devotional readers, fracking the tale suggests that its truth is universal. Addiction in general and alcoholism in particular are behind many of our most frightening statistics. The consequences for families living in the shadow of addiction are far-reaching.

PART TWO

Living with Challenges

7

Gabriel

Matthew 1:18–25, Luke 1:5–38

IN THE CHRISTIAN TRADITION, nothing has inspired anything like midrash in the way that the Christmas story has. Imaginative piety has had a field day with the stories from Matthew and Luke's Gospels. From the little drummer boy who wound his way into the ranks of the shepherds to the gifts of three astrologers who morphed into three kings with names and distinct ethnic backgrounds, the wonderful story has been stretched in almost every conceivable direction. Is there any place yet to go, any character yet to be analyzed? In spite of all that has been written, painted, and dramatized, I think one character in the story still deserves fresh consideration. Consider the Archangel Gabriel, God's messenger who approached both the mother of Jesus and the father of John the Baptist at the beginning of the story. Gabriel only appears in the most elaborate of Christmas Pageants, but his role as God's messenger is essential to the drama.

Because angels in general and Gabriel in particular are not in the mainstream of contemporary piety, it may be helpful to set them in context before fracking the Christmas texts. For most of us, angels are cute cartoon figures, which reflects our arrogant tendency to make jokes out of ancient wisdom. Before we write them off, however, we might note that Jesus clearly believed in angels, as did virtually everyone else in those days. Those who maintain that Jesus knew everything about God but was hallucinating when he spoke of angels are on thin ice, logically and theologically. The word *angel* means *messenger*. An *archangel* is a *chief messenger*. Their traditional role includes acting as God's connecting link with human beings, which is how we meet Gabriel in the Christmas story.

When this archangel is depicted at all, it is usually as part of the Annunciation, telling Mary that she will conceive and bear a son who will be the Redeemer. Mary is held in high and proper esteem for her obedient response: "Here am I, the servant of the Lord; let it be with me according to your word." We can begin fracking the story at that response. If Mary is to be honored for accepting Gabriel's invitation, she must have had the option to turn him down. No one is credited for obeying the law of gravity because there is no choice. The same is true of aging and dying. Without an option to refuse, obedience means nothing, so Gabriel was extending an invitation rather than announcing a *fait accompli*; if not, Mary deserves more pity than praise.

The possibility of refusal allows us to wonder if Mary of Nazareth was the first person the archangel asked. Perhaps there was a Mary of Bethlehem. Having her serve as the mother of Jesus would at least have had the logistical advantage of avoiding the necessity to move a pregnant woman seventy miles in order to fulfill the prophecy of the messiah coming from the city of King David's birth. For whatever reasons, it is possible that Gabriel approached Mary of Bethlehem and was turned down. Why might she do that?

In her understanding of the universe, the appearance of an angel would have been frighteningly rare, but certainly possible and more likely than in our way of thinking. While popular cosmology has changed, human nature has not. The idea of presenting oneself as pregnant with no father other than the Holy Spirit would be a daunting prospect in any age. If she were betrothed—as Mary of Nazareth was—it would involve an incredibly awkward conversation with her intended, and no guarantee of the outcome, as Matthew records in his telling of the story. Sharing the news with her parents would have been even more challenging, as her virginity represented a substantial investment. If she married well, the family would benefit. If she were "damaged goods" for want of virginity, she would be a liability dependent on her birth family for the rest of her life. Facing her loved ones with the vague promise that the child to be born "will be great" would have been cold comfort. It is not difficult to understand hypothetical Mary of Bethlehem's refusal.

Many of us have known clearly what God wants us to do but turned away because the immediate and tangible consequences seemed to outweigh the long-term possibilities. Understanding the refusal of Mary of Bethlehem makes admiration for Mary of Nazareth even greater. For that reason, the latter Mary enjoys a large and enthusiastic following who try to model their lives on her obedience. It is not imprudent to suggest that Mary of Bethlehem has an even larger (though less public) following: people who model their lives after her example; people who have seen the possible consequences of faithfulness and said, "No thank you."

If Gabriel were refused by Mary of Bethlehem, his attention would have turned to Plan B, Mary of Nazareth. Before setting out on the journey north, the archangel made a stop in the nearby temple in Jerusalem. There he found an elderly priest named Zechariah offering incense in the sanctuary. Having barren women give birth was one of God's signature events (Isaac born to Sarah, Samuel born to Hannah). Zechariah's childless wife Elizabeth was to be next in line. Their child was destined to be the Elijah of Jewish expectation, the herald of God's Messiah. Christians would know him as John the Baptist. When Gabriel gave Zechariah the good news, the old man responded with doubt rather than the expected joy. "How will I know that this is so? I am an old man and my wife is getting on in years." With Mary of Bethlehem's refusal still ringing in his ears, the archangel did not handle the priest's questions gently. "I am Gabriel! I stand in the presence of God! . . . I have been sent to bring you this good news. But now because you did not believe my words . . . you will become mute . . . until the day these things occur" (Luke 1:8–20). It was a frustrating day for the archangel.

One can imagine him returning to the heavenly precincts and venting his exasperations with his fellow angels. Overhearing the tirade, I suspect that God called Gabriel aside to explain that humans are not at all like angels. Whereas angels are swift to obey God's command, humans only do so slowly, after debate and a vigorous search for alternatives. God may have reminded him of the story of Jonah and all that it took to get that man to warn the people of Nineveh, and how he then perversely resented his own success. It may have been necessary to point out that humans have a limited grasp of reality coupled with an almost unlimited confidence in their own viewpoint. These characteristics are precisely why God was coming among them in the flesh; not only to tell them but show them the way things really are; to give them an opportunity to live in God's reality instead of their own delusion. The refusal of Mary of Bethlehem and the doubt of Zechariah were not failures of Gabriel's mission, they were actually the reasons for it.

Gabriel, being an angel, took the admonition to heart. When he delivered God's message to Mary of Nazareth, she responded with the same doubt that Zechariah had expressed: "How can this be, since I am a virgin?" This time, however, instead of blowing up, the angel could not have been nicer: "The Holy Spirit will come upon you . . . the child to be born will be called . . . the Son of God." He offered her God's unique sign: "your relative Elizabeth in her old age has also conceived . . . For nothing will be impossible with God."

The idea that an angel could be frustrated may seem farfetched until one remembers that they are responsible for conveying God's messages to human beings. Even an angel is bound to find that frustrating from time to time.

8

John the Baptist

Matthew 3; Mark 1; Luke 1, 3; John 1

IF THE LANGUAGE OF fashion can be used in the study of theology and Scripture, it could be said that Jesus and his second cousin John were "bespoke"; in other words, made to order. Their birth was heralded by the Archangel Gabriel as unique and specific acts of God—John to "make ready a people prepared for the Lord" and Jesus to "be called the Son of the Most High . . . to reign over the house of Jacob forever." The stories are well-remembered in Advent and rendered in every possible form at Christmas, providing a familiarity that can easily overlook some sticking points. A thoughtful reading of John's story indicates that, while he fulfilled his role of preparing people for the coming of the Messiah, he apparently misunderstood the Messiah he was proclaiming. Is it possible to serve God's purposes while being mistaken about what those purposes might be? Fracking John's story allows us to understand him in fresh ways and to wonder anew about how the plan of God sometimes unfolds.

The little we know about John provides enticing possibilities for understanding him. His father Zechariah's incredulous response to Gabriel's prediction of John's birth was "I am an old man and my wife is getting on in years." Their advanced age allows the possibility that John was orphaned while young and could have been given a home by a religious community, like the Essenes or "Pious Ones" in the Judean desert. Any connection between John and the Essenes is speculative, but well within the scope of biblical fracking. Both were radically ascetic, wilderness-based, keen on the coming of God's Messiah, and used a form of baptism as a sign of repentance. These similarities may explain John's appearance, dress, and diet, and it would not be beyond possible to think that the early loss of his parents might account for some of the anger that so clearly characterized him. And somewhere along the way he gained an insight that was denied most of his contemporaries.

John understood that God and God's Messiah were focused on the faithful and how they met the demands of belief. The great majority of John's contemporaries expected the messiah to be a military-political leader who would free Israel from foreign occupation. John knew otherwise, and called the nation to radical faithfulness, generosity, and responsibility. He dismissed the pretensions that came from being inheritors of God's promises to Abraham and was scornful of the rank and prestige that society confers. Religious leaders were a "brood of vipers" and King Herod was taken to task for his marital misconduct. When John mentioned Rome at all, it was to address the excesses of common soldiers rather than the designs of rulers. John knew where God's eyes were fixed, and it was not on the nation of Israel, but on the people of Israel.

John was also convinced of God's reaction to what he saw. It was outrage. Like so many prophets before him, John took that conviction to heart and made it his own. He knew, beyond a shadow of doubt, that God's anger was about to blaze a trail through Israel the likes of which had not been seen before. The axe was at hand, the winnowing fork was poised, the waters of fiery baptism were coming to a boil.

Anger like John's has a complicated root system because it is not just his own frustration, but God's. That meant that John was not free to mitigate, compromise, or forgive on his own. Righteous anger like his is unrelenting, takes no prisoners, and allows no exceptions, largely because its human representatives lack the authority to relent, reprieve, or except. The source of their outrage is rooted beyond and above them; in God or patriotism, tradition or victims who cannot speak for themselves—the list of possibilities is extensive. When a person's anger is righteous in this sense, he simply cannot let go on its own. Understanding the severe limits of righteous anger is the key to understanding the strange role John played in God's plan of salvation.

The Gospels are clear that John recognized Jesus as the promised Messiah. They are also clear about John's expectations of how his cousin's messianic role would be carried out: with blood and thunder. Jesus would be like John, only more powerful. He would separate what good wheat there was from all of the useless chaff. He would levy unquenchable fire on the multitudes, not Pentecost's uniting tongues of flame but the scourging blazes of Revelation. That much was clear to John, but it was not to be the case.

John's blanket condemnations got him in trouble with King Herod's wife Herodias, who pressured the king into arresting the wilderness prophet. From Herod's dungeon, John waited for word of the beginning of Jesus' messianic rampage. The reports he received, however, were of healings, not burnings; demons cast out rather than unleashed; parables told, feasts attended, and children blessed. There were sharp disputes with Pharisees, but no swaths of destruction. How could that be? He had been sure Jesus was the Messiah; the vision at his baptism confirmed it. But why was he not behaving like a messiah? Could John have miscalculated? He sent messengers to Jesus, asking, "Are you the one who is to come or are we to wait for another?" The reply spun the concept of God's plan completely around. "Go and tell John what you have seen and heard: the blind receive their sight, the lame walk, the lepers are cleansed, the deaf hear, the dead are raised, the poor have good news brought to them." Then Jesus added what must have been a pointed message to John: "And blessed is anyone who takes no offense at me" (Luke 7:18–23).

What was going on? Had John been wrong? I don't think so. He was right, but only for a short period of time.

Anger can play a valuable role in life. It clarifies by sweeping away nuance and focusing on what is wrong. Anger creates energy and forces decisions out of reluctant fence sitters. In many situations, it is sinful not to be angry, as when injustice and cruelty hold sway. Anger is like a bulldozer that clears a building lot. It is an essential step, but no one builds anything permanent with bulldozers. They play their role and then must make way for the more subtle and supple arts of construction. That was John's part in the salvation story, clearing the way for the Messiah. In order to play it well, he had to believe it fully, which he did. His anger was as genuine as it was righteous. But while anger is often right and necessary, it is rarely enough for the long term, and it is terribly difficult to let go of once it has done its work. For John, letting go proved impossible.

God's salvation plan was about forgiveness, reconciliation, and joy. John's attention-getting anger helped the people of Israel to recognize their need for those things, but it could not provide them. John, like Jesus, was bespoke, and like Jesus he did what he was called to do. He prepared for the kingdom, but he could not build it. That is why Jesus said, "I tell you, among those born of women no one is greater than John; yet the least in the kingdom of God is greater than he" (Luke 7:28).

9

The Rich Young Man

Mark 10:17–31

THOSE WHO STUDY CONTEMPORARY issues tell us we are particularly averse to contradiction. We limit ourselves to news sources and opinions with which we already agree. We live, we are told, in various "news bubbles" where we seek and find not information but confirmation. Consequently, our views are deeply rooted but rarely enriched, firmly held but seldom expanded. The scholars may be right about us, but if so, we are far from the first to prefer continuing affirmation over new evidence. Fracking the story of Jesus and the rich young man may provide some insight into that story as well as our own.

The rich man (Matthew tells us he was young) was supremely confident of his standing in God's eyes. Popular theology equated temporal wealth with divine approval. It is, on examination, a seriously flawed belief. Exceptions abound as the wicked often prosper while the righteous suffer. The Psalms, especially 37 and 73, question it, and the book of Job tears it to shreds, but people were then (and are still today) drawn to its clarity and simplicity. It is an absurdity, like our assumptions that people who are famous for one thing are wise about other things, that beautiful people are more interesting than others, or that young people with mature bodies have mature minds. Evidence to the contrary has little effect on such popular beliefs. As one might imagine, the prosperous are especially devoted to the idea that good things are a measure of good lives.

It was in the false but happy glow of this flawed belief that the rich man approached Jesus. It is worth noting, as Mark does, that the encounter took place as Jesus was setting out on a journey. People who expect quick and easy answers to complex questions often bring them up when serious conversation is unlikely. Clergy will recognize those who ask meaning-of-life questions at receptions or in receiving lines when no more than a bumper sticker bromide is possible. The idea is to avoid complexity and cut to the simple sought-after answer. As was so often the case, Jesus moved the conversation from the expected to the unexpected.

The man greeted Jesus as "Good Teacher," perhaps counting on the goodness of Jesus to recognize the goodness of the wealthy petitioner. Disturbingly, Jesus did not accept the accolade, but connected eternal life to obeying God's law. "No problem," countered the man, "I always obey God's law."

Mark tells us the Teacher then looked at him, an unusual detail in the usually sparse descriptions of Mark's Gospel. How long did Jesus pause to look at him as the preparations for his journey went on hold? Did their eyes lock? Did Jesus see a puppy-like vulnerability, laid open by easy belief in a false assumption? The man only wanted to be told that he was good in God's eyes. Could he handle a heavy dose of reality? It would be so easy for Jesus to give him the verbal equivalent of a hug and send him on his innocent way. But Jesus loved him, and the love of Jesus is inextricably bound up in reality.

The reality was that the young man had mixed up what he thought were the signs of God's love with the responsibilities that love laid upon him. His wealth constituted the tools of his response to God's love, not the love itself. The real love of God is a way of giving, not getting. It is something one lives into, not off of. And if life is really eternal, it includes this phase as well as the next. The eternal life the man sought to inherit is not waiting beyond the grave, but is here and now. The rich young man was asking for affirmation of a flawed, self-serving worldview. He wanted to be told he had arrived, when he was actually just starting. Unfortunately for him, love in reality is often a harsh thing when compared to love in dreams, and "from everyone to whom much is given much is required" (Luke 12:48). Jesus loved him, literally *really* loved him, so he told him the truth and ruined his day.

Mark tells us the man went away "grieving." How might that have played out? What do people do when sought-after affirmation becomes disturbing contradiction? Did he grapple with what Jesus was trying to tell him, or did he retreat into the comforting confidence of his previous assumptions? Did he insist that Jesus did not understand how things are, how complex wealth can be, how many people relied on his success? Did the embarrassment of being put down while so many people were watching convince him that Jesus was cruel and persecuting him? Perhaps Jesus was even jealous of his good life. Or did he try to see himself apart from his possessions; as a child of God, dependent on grace rather than goods, service rather than surplus? Jesus let the man walk away with an incredible burden to sort through. Did he, after a few steps, turn back and try to ask Jesus some follow-up questions, only to find that the Good Teacher had left on his journey, and he had to figure things out for himself?

Mark tells us that, after the encounter, Jesus talked about how hard it is for wealthy people to grasp the kingdom of God, how difficult it is to separate the stuff of this world from the fruits of the Spirit. It is so hard that his disciples, who did not have much stuff, could not imagine it. Which led Jesus to declare that "For mortals it is impossible, but not for God; for God, all things are possible." That Zen-like truth was not what the young man was looking for; it is difficult to grasp while confidently holding a self-serving view.

10

Nicodemus

John 3, 7, 19

JOHN, THE AUTHOR OF the Gospel and the book of Revelation, makes wonderful use of symbolic language. In his wise and careful hands, common words and images carry vast and complex meanings. Few are more weighted than "light"/"day" and "dark"/"night." The former denotes righteousness, belief, and a relationship with God. The latter signifies evil, unbelief, and separation from God. Recognizing that John chooses his symbolic words carefully provides a beginning point for fracking the story of Nicodemus, the high-ranking Pharisee who approached Jesus seeking a better understanding of what he was about. Most people know the story as the lead-in to a favorite passage: "For God so loved the world that he gave his only Son, so that everyone who believes in him may not perish but have everlasting life" (3:16). Fracking takes us in a different direction.

John is the only source of information about Nicodemus, but the picture is compelling. He was not only a Pharisee, a member of the most respected and rigorous religious group in first-century Israel, but a member of the Sanhedrin, the closest the occupied nation had to a governing body. To say he was part of the Establishment would be an understatement, and one would not be faulted for thinking that he would be leery of challengers to the status quo like Jesus of Nazareth. But Nicodemus had another quality besides spiritual discipline, legal expertise, and political ability. He apparently had an open mind, an attribute rare at any time but almost unheard of in his day. That openness led him from inquiry to open debate to defiant action. Not only did he seek a private conversation with Jesus, but he took up for him before the Sanhedrin and joined Joseph of Arimathea in claiming his body on Good Friday, an act that rendered him unclean for the Passover rituals as well as politically isolated in the Sanhedrin. It is not difficult to admire one defined by those qualities and characterized by those actions, especially when twenty centuries of reflection support his conclusions.

But John opens a door to serious fracking when he tells us that Nicodemus originally came to Jesus "by night," implying a lack of righteousness, belief, and a broken relationship with God. Current religious thinking values the seeker and honors those who go to some trouble to learn about, if not directly from, different religious views. But apparently John did not see it that way. The Gospel writer did not have the word in his vocabulary, but in our terms he was fracking Nicodemus. I doubt that he knew the Pharisee personally, but determined the darkness of his state of mind through speculative imagination. What might John have seen that modern readers would miss?

The dialogue in John 3 is intended to reveal the mind of Jesus, so Nicodemus's thinking comes only by inference. Even with that limitation, it seems apparent that the inquirer was trying to fit Jesus' new teaching into a preexisting framework. When Jesus spoke of being "born from above," Nicodemus tried to tie the idea to physical birth. When Jesus told about the swirling mystery of the Holy Spirit, Nicodemus tried to understand it logically, and had to give up with "How can this be?" Admirable as the inquiry might be, the inquirer was hopelessly unprepared to lay hold of the answer. Jesus would say in another context that new wine needs new wineskins (Mark 2:22). Nicodemus was standing at a veritable fountain of new wine, holding nothing but an old wineskin.

It did not work because it could never work. The wind cannot be caught in a net, love cannot be required in a contract, wisdom does not automatically come with a diploma, and new truth does not readily conform to old understandings. As long as Nicodemus was trying to fit the good news into an old framework, it was night, the kind of spiritual darkness John deplores, and it would remain so until he began to really, simply, and completely hear what Jesus was saying.

That is a very difficult thing to do. It does not mean that everything that was understood and accepted before has to be discarded for what is new. What it does mean is that the inquirer needs to do some theological downsizing, looking closely at what has been important to see if it will be important in the context of a new reality. Just as homeowners headed for apartment living need to assess the continued role of the dining room table and vacation souvenirs, theological seekers must know the difference between essential truth and cultural comforts, between the truths time has hallowed and those it has left behind.

Downsizing, physically as well as theologically, is a difficult task. It requires a cold eye and a willingness to let go of what has been good in order to take hold of that which is supposed to be better. Religious seekers like Nicodemus must wrestle with the fact that faith traditions are always a combination of what God reveals and what people in a certain time, place, and culture develop to interpret to that revelation. Nicodemus's orthodox world had established rigid protocols for righteousness, belief, and a relationship with God. A great deal of Jesus' teaching was in opposition to that way of thinking, so his disciple John readily saw it as darkness. But the highly placed Pharisee whose life, career, and faith had been based on mastery of those protocols certainly would have to struggle with the distinction. Indeed, it is remarkable that he would bother to struggle with it at all.

Was Nicodemus successful? Was he able to think his way into a new truth? There is, of course, no way to know for certain. We cannot know his mind, but we do know something of his actions. And when one comes down to it, actions are clearer than thoughts, for they lack the qualifying exceptions and nuanced interpretations of language, especially theological language. As noted, John tells us that Nicodemus spoke up when his Sanhedrin colleagues began to railroad Jesus without due process (7:50–52), and that on Good Friday he helped claim and bury the Lord's body (19:39). Those actions tell a story worth noting.

The dividing line between God's revelation and the human constructs designed to receive it are often blurred for us. But behavior that purports to serve the divine while actually protecting the human is easier to recognize. When courts of justice become instruments of injustice; when institutions of learning begin to distort truth; when those in positions of trust become predators; when those responsible for public safety become dangerous, the dividing line becomes clear, and it is time to amend the temporal institutions so that the greater truths can be served. While he may or may not have comprehended the full truth of Jesus's teaching, Nicodemus did recognize the injustice deployed against it and the need for compassion at its apparent end. Those actions on behalf of God's greater and deeper expectations for humanity are a profound form of faith, worthy of the brightest light and the clearest day.

11

Judas Iscariot

Matthew 26–27; Mark 14; Luke 22; John 13, 18

THE TRIAL OF JUDAS is over; the guilty verdict has been rendered by Gospel writers, history, and Judas himself. Because of that, to say that Iscariot has suffered from bad press is a gross understatement. His name has become a curse and an insult. At first glance, the possibility of discovering anything new seems slight at best, but it may prove to be the richest of all. History's judgment of Judas has made him so bad that we have lost all empathy with him. When we allow the actors in the crucifixion drama, including Judas, to become one-dimensional cutouts, we lose our connection with the universal power of the event.

What was Judas's role in Good Friday? He betrayed Jesus, apparently for the paltry sum of thirty pieces of silver, about five weeks wages. But if that were his motivation, why did he try to return it? And if he actually sought the death of Jesus, why did he respond to that success by committing suicide? There is more going on than popular disdain can convey, but which fracking may help us discover.

To successfully revisit the case of Judas, we must go behind the interpretations of the Gospel writers, who wrote thirty to seventy years after the events they describe. The convictions that grew out of Easter had already hardened and made it difficult for the faithful to remember the understandings and turmoil that guided the principal characters in their actions. It requires some agility of the mind to see the events of Holy Week as contemporaries must have seen them.

To reach that pre-Easter mindset, we must begin with the thing that *everybody* knew beyond a shadow of a doubt: The Messiah was to be a political-military figure who would lead a rebellion against Rome and restore the kingdom of David. The central theme of Jerusalem's Holy Week was rebellion, not resurrection. Everyone was concerned with either starting or preventing the former; no one had a clue about the latter.

Rebellion was not just the pipe dream of angry citizens or the paranoia of officials. The most recent rebellion had been under the Maccabees, who successfully threw out the Greeks 160 years before (about the same length of time as from our Civil War to the present), but the memory of that wisp of glory was kept fresh by the hard fact of Roman occupation that began about 60 BCE. The actual rebellion everyone expected would take place in 70 CE— four decades later—leading to the Jewish diaspora, which lasted until 1948. The focus on revolution was well-justified.

How do we know this was the preoccupation during the original Holy Week? The last question anyone ever asked Jesus on earth was, "Lord, is this the time when you will restore the kingdom to Israel?" (Acts 1:6). That innocent inquiry came after all of the Holy Week events, including Easter, and the resurrection appearances. The questioner, who is mercifully not named, is basically saying that Holy Week and Easter have been swell, but when are we going to get to the heart of the matter and rebel against the Romans!

The High Priest Caiaphas gave this reason for the crucifixion: "[I]t is better for one man to die . . . than to have the whole nation destroyed" (John 11:50). That is good reasoning, but why would the nation be destroyed? It is because they expected that man to start the revolution, the one that did start thirty-five years later.

The threat of rebellion was the reason Pilate came up from Caesarea on the coast with his legions. The certainty about a political/military messiah was the reason Peter rebuked Jesus when Jesus spoke of dying and rising again (Matt 16:22). James and John had a restored political kingdom of David in mind when they asked Jesus if they could be on his right and left hands when he came into his kingdom (Mark 10:35–45).

Jesus did talk about crucifixion and resurrection, but his words were like the warning about the O-ring on the Challenger spacecraft. After it crashed, people reread the material and found the warnings they should have heeded. But at the time, those words, like many prophetic messages, were lost in the long process of unfolding life. Lest we judge them too harshly, it is worth noting that contemporary scholars still do not agree on the meaning of the kingdom of God, the crucifixion, or the resurrection.

With an understanding of the central concern of everyone except Jesus, let us look closely at Judas. He was one of the Twelve, a member of the inner circle. In addition, he was trusted with the common purse (John 13:29). Consider what the Holy Week beginning on Palm Sunday looked like to Judas and his fellow disciples. Jesus entered on a donkey, which we all know to be a sign of peace in fulfillment of prophecy (Zech 9:9), but John tells us that the disciples did not understand these things until after Easter (John 12:16). The crowds and disciples' acclamation of "Hosanna to the Son of David" would have been the clearer message: This is the political/military figure just like David!

As we know, Jesus went to the temple and drove out the money changers. Whatever else might have been involved in that endeavor, the crowd would have noticed that it was the first violent act by Jesus, the very kind of behavior that a revolutionary has to exhibit. Undoubtedly, they would have preferred violence directed to the Roman garrison attached to the temple courtyard, but routing the money changers would have been pretty exciting in itself.

When we look at Monday, Tuesday, and Wednesday through the lens of those expecting a political/military messiah, it appears that Jesus had an edge at the beginning, but wasted it in the next three days. Instead of building on the enthusiasm of Palm Sunday, he spent his days in temple debates with Sadducees and Pharisees and his evenings in Bethany with Lazarus, Mary, and Martha. It would be as if the United States intervened in a war zone by establishing a Center for Women's Rights. It would be nice, but hardly what anyone felt they needed.

Wednesday night would have been the turning point. All of the gospels tell the story. John describes it this way:

> Six days before the Passover, Jesus came to Bethany, the home of Lazarus, whom he had raised from the dead. There they gave a dinner for him. Martha served, and Lazarus was one of those at the table with him. Mary took a pound of costly perfume made of pure nard, anointed Jesus' feet, and wiped them with her hair. The house was filled with the fragrance of the perfume. But Judas Iscariot, one of his disciples (the one who was about to betray him), said "Why was this perfume not sold for three hundred denarii and the money given to the poor?" (John 12:1–11)

It was the straw that broke the camel's back. Jesus was betraying the revolution, not just by ignoring the crowd and the Romans, but now by lapping up the extravagant devotion of this woman. He clearly needed to be brought back "on message" and away from the distractions of excessive feminine devotion. How could Judas get him back on track?

The solution was to set up his capture by playing on the temple authorities' fear of revolution. If he were captured, Jesus would have to fight. But how might Judas convince the authorities to spring his trap? He could not say it was to force Jesus to begin a rebellion, because the temple authorities were trying to prevent that, as Caiaphas indicated. The answer was to provide a motive everyone would understand: money. Thirty pieces of silver. It was a failsafe plan. Either Jesus would get back to the business at hand and be the messiah everyone knew he should be, or he was a fraud who was leading them all away from what they knew to be God's intent—the restoration of the kingdom of David. If that were the case, the law is clear:

> If prophets or those who divine by dreams appear among
> you and promise you omens or portents, *and the omens*
> *or the portents declared by them take place,* and they say,
> *"Let us follow other gods" (whom you have not known)*
> "and let us serve them," you must not heed the words of
> those prophets or those who divine by dreams; for the
> LORD your God is testing you, to know whether you
> indeed love the LORD your God with all your heart and
> soul . . . But *those prophets or those who divine by dreams*
> *shall be put to death* for having spoken treason against
> the LORD your God . . . So you shall purge the evil from
> your midst. (Deut 13:1–5; emphasis added)

If Jesus were in fact a false messiah, the law condemned him to
death!

Why didn't Judas realize what Jesus was really about at the
Last Supper when the acts and symbols were made so clear? How
did he miss the message about God's grace and servant leadership?

We must remember that the evening included several recorded events that would not have been priorities for the disciples.
The primary symbol would have been Passover, the recollection
of God's intervention on behalf of Israel to free them from Egyptian domination, the very thing the revolutionary messiah was
supposed to do. Bread and wine were reinterpreted, but not with
any clarity (as can be seen in that Christians today still debate the
meaning). During the evening, Jesus foretold his betrayal, to which
every disciple asked, "Is it I?"— a question that only makes sense if
the potential for betrayal was very real. Judas was not the only one
re-considering his loyalty to Jesus. There was an argument about
who was greatest, and Peter bragged about loyalty. Jesus washed
their feet and deepened their confusion.

Luke 22:35–38 tells us of this exchange at the supper: He said
to them, "When I sent you out without a purse, bag, or sandals, did
you lack anything?" They said, "No, not a thing." He said to them,
"But now, the one who has a purse must take it, and likewise a bag.
And the one who has no sword must sell his cloak and buy one.
For I tell you, this scripture must be fulfilled in me, 'And he was
counted among the lawless'; and indeed what is written about me

is being fulfilled." They said, "Lord, look, here are two swords." He replied, "It is enough."

What would "It is enough" mean to the disciples bent on revolution? I do not know what Jesus meant by it, but I can guess what the disciples heard in it. I believe they would have remembered the feeding miracles when a couple of loaves and few fish fed a multitude. That same power could turn two swords into an arsenal.

Thursday would have been more impressive for its promise of rebellion through Passover patriotism and sword talk than its emphasis on servant leadership and sacrifice through foot washing. I think Judas would have been encouraged by the fact that everyone in the room identified with the possibility of betrayal. I think he would have been confused by the bread imagery and disgusted by the foot washing. Neither were appropriate for a revolutionary leader.

Fracking suggests that Judas was convinced that, once Jesus was seized by the temple authorities, he would call on God for divine intervention. That intervention was the secret weapon in the revolutionaries' arsenal. Matthew tells us, however, that when Jesus was arrested, "Suddenly, one of those with Jesus put his hand on his sword, drew it, and struck the slave of the high priest, cutting off his ear. Then Jesus said to him, "Put your sword back into its place; for all who take the sword will perish by the sword. Do you think that I cannot appeal to my Father, and he will at once send me more than twelve legions of angels?" (Matt 26:51–53).

When those angels, or their equivalent, were not forthcoming, Judas's carefully laid plan began to unravel.

How do we know that Judas did not intend for Jesus to be killed? His remorse is proof enough. Suicide is not a common way to celebrate success. He wanted Jesus to fight, not to die. But why not let the Law in Deuteronomy be fulfilled?

Perhaps Judas got a glimpse—the barest of glimpses, but a glimpse nonetheless—into what Jesus' messiahship was all about. Judas took his own life after Jesus' death, but before his resurrection, so he did not see the whole story. The part that he did see was Jesus accepting death as part of something larger than life. He saw a martyr, a word that means "witness," but witnessing to what? Perhaps he realized that Jesus never spoke of the kingdom of David, but only the kingdom of God. Perhaps he sensed that political kingdoms are by nature self-centered and self-serving, and that a kingdom of God would be just the opposite—other-centered and self-giving. Maybe he realized that his understanding of Jesus and the act of betrayal that grew out of that understanding were not only wrong, but absolutely backward. If that is true, then Judas the betrayer is, in rudimentary form, the first believer. The crucifixion crushed him, which is what Good Friday without Easter would do to anyone.

12

Onesiphorus and Ananias

2 Timothy 1:15–19; Acts 9:1–19

COMPASSION IS, FOR THE most part, reactive. We see a person in need, and we do something about it. There must be a special place in heaven for those whose compassion is proactive; those who sense rather than see a need, who take the risks inherent in knocking on silent doors, who give before they are asked, who go beyond the dictates of common goodness. They can, of course, be gloriously wrong in their assumptions, violate the boundaries of their neighbors, and come across as meddlesome busybodies; but when they are right, glory shines among us. Here are two personifications of proactive compassion: Onesiphorous not only supported Paul in prison, but sought him out to do so; Ananias went to the apostle when his lethal danger to Christians was still widely known. Fracking their stories can help open our eyes to the possibilities and dangers of following their examples.

Onesiphorous ("On-e-**siph**-o-rus") is hardly a household name, but perhaps it should be. His single reference is in the letter Paul wrote to Timothy from his confinement in Rome. In it the apostle laments that everybody in Asia has turned against him. The one exception is Onesiphorous, who "refreshed" him in spite of his chains. What is more, the good man came to Rome and searched for Paul until he found him, which in a city without street names or addresses must have been a daunting task. Why would he do that for someone so unpopular? I doubt it was personal. If Saint Paul spent any time in charm school, his epistles do not indicate it. Even Barnabas, easily the most generous-hearted man in the Bible, gave up on the cranky apostle. It is one thing to leave one's door open to someone like Paul. It is something else to go knocking on doors to find him. Why would anyone take that extra step?

If one looks for external reasons to seek out Paul at what was obviously the end of his life and ministry, the view is barren. Paul could return no favors, advance no causes, reward no gestures. Onesiphorous's motivation had to be internal, a particular kind of compassion, one that flew in the face of popular sentiment and took no counsel from prudence or expediency. I believe One-siphorous was what we might call a compassionate contrarian, one who identifies with those whom society shuns. In school, he went unerringly to the unattractive kid eating lunch alone. At work, his productivity was constantly interrupted by "checking on" those around him. In the rat race of life, his eyes were always on the back of the pack, looking for those lagging behind or dropping out. Admirable as his compassion may have been, it was not always wise, or even helpful. He often took his signals from the majority, assuming they were wrong in distancing themselves from anyone. But sometimes people belong alone so they can reflect on their life choices. Others prefer to be separated from the community and view the outstretched hand as a threat to their solitude. And, of course, some are deeply wounded, unready for even a well-intended embrace. Paul could have been any of these and more. It is hard to tell what might happen to a person like Paul who is switched from active to passive, independent to dependent, care-giver to care-receiver.

In this case, Onesiphorous got it right. Saint Paul was touched, moved, and grateful for his efforts. But how did he know the apos-tle would welcome him? I think Onesiphorous made a calculated guess. He considered what he knew: Paul was once a leader, now abandoned; once free, now in chains. The compassionate contrarian did not simply follow his kneejerk goodness, but figured that what Paul lost was human contact, so some response from a human, any human, would be welcome. How did he "refresh" Paul? Simply by showing up. Onesiphorous had no key to unlock the chains, no convening power to bring back Paul's lost followers. He found the right door, knocked, and waited to see what would happen next. Sometimes just showing up is all that is needed. Sometimes it is so important that it is worth combing the twisted streets of Rome to make it happen.

Ananias's compassion was in a different category. As with Onesiphorous, his story is about reaching out to Paul when he was in trouble. While on his way to Damascus to hunt for Christians, Paul had a dramatic and mysterious encounter with Christ that left him blind and confused. Some will maintain that Paul's blindness was not physical, but a metaphor for his confusion. That is worth noting, but it does not change Ananias's story. The book of Acts tells us that Ananias encountered the Lord in a vision and heard Jesus instruct him to find Paul and help him regain his sight. The exchange is simple: Ananias was not enthusiastic, but the Lord said, "Go anyway," so Ananias went. We can begin fracking at that point of vision/dialog.

There is nothing wrong with taking the story at face value. There was something to see (vision) and something to hear (dialogue). If that is the case, Ananias's courageous walk to the street called Straight had a dramatic boost that is denied to most of us, and his story is not much like our own. But if his story is like mine and perhaps yours, there was not as much clarity as the biblical account implies.

Common experience includes communications that the faithful readily attribute to God. For the most part, those experiences do not include the kind of auditory moments that are the essence of human conversation. One does not as often "hear" God as realize one has "heard" God. God's idea simply turns up in our heads without any reliance on our ears. It is more likely to be described as insight or impulse than as vison or conversation, but it is the Lord nonetheless. Unfortunately, we sinful human beings have many insights and impulses that are not from God, so the faithful, especially the proactively compassionate faithful like Ananias, have to do some sorting.

How does one distinguish between divine commissions and ridiculous ideas? If there were a foolproof method, faithfulness would be a lot easier than it is, but there are some options. I believe that Ananias not only knew God, he knew something about the interests of God; he knew the sort of things God wants in his world and from his people. He knew that God is forgiving and, from the examples of Jesus, readily reaches across lines of propriety, expectation, and even common sense to offer it. He had heard about Paul and his confused vulnerability, and he had the notion that he should reach out to him, so he went.

Here the stories of Onesiphorous and Ananias come together. The journey from the quiet safety of prayerfully wondering what to do to and actually knocking on Paul's door must have been long, anxious, and daunting. God's clarity, like the warmth of an open fire, becomes more of a memory than a feeling as we walk away into the cold reality of human interaction. The voices of reason keep whispering that we are crazy to be doing this. Paul, like a trapped animal, might not know rescuer from predator; he might not know if his visitors have come for good or ill. All Onesiphorous, Ananias, and those who follow them can know is that they are doing the sort of thing God wants done. Being faithful the way God expects and being successful the way the world understands are not always the same thing. Being faithful often looks a lot like being foolish and, to be honest, attempts at being faithful sometimes turn out to be foolish. There are no guarantees. Yet Onesiphorous and Ananias kept going, and the glory of God shone through them.

Being proactively compassionate requires a rich and generous heart, along with an informed and critical mind. Onesiphorous and Ananias both took risks, but they were calculated risks. Faithful reckoning is as essential to living in the kingdom of God as faithful risk-taking.

PART THREE

Living in Community

13

Eliezer and Justus

Genesis 15:2; Acts 1:21–26

"VIRTUE IS ITS OWN reward" is a familiar saying commonly applied as salve for other people's disappointments, but rarely experienced as satisfying when applied to one's own. As the biblical story unfolds into history, there were many joyful saints and more than a few hardworking souls who were left with the cold comfort of unrequited virtue. The latter are so common among us and their experience is so basic to our own lives that fracking their story requires very little conjecture. Eliezer of Damascus and Joseph, aka Barsabbas, aka Justus, are two who have borne the burdens of disappointment and worn the stoic countenance of the Not Chosen.

Some 1800 years before the birth of Christ, the patriarch Abram was promised by God that he would be the father of a great nation. It was on the strength of this promise that his name was changed from Abram, meaning Exalted Ancestor, to Abraham, meaning Ancestor of a Multitude. As all who live by God's promise know, it is hard to get the Eternal God to hurry up. The promise of an heir was delayed—long delayed. Abraham could hear his own biological clock ticking, and was aware that his wife Sarah's had run down altogether. In his anxiety, the aging patriarch lamented to God, "I continue childless and the heir to my house is Eliezer of Damascus . . . a slave born in my house is to be my heir."

An entry point for fracking the story is that if Abraham thought his servant would inherit his estate, Eliezer undoubtedly thought so too. That possibility probably adopted the guise of certainty, as attractive possibilities are wont to do. It is not difficult to peer into Eliezer's mind and see him planning how he would run things when he was in charge. Just before going to sleep at night, he undoubtedly enjoyed arranging the furniture of his very bright future, living into the fantasy that was to become his reality. It is the sort of thing we all do when the doorway to a bright future stands so tantalizingly ajar. We may not say it out loud to others, but we *know* the job will be ours, the beloved will say "Yes," the gamble will pay off.

But it was not to be. Abraham and Sarah finally did have the long-delayed miracle baby. They were so overjoyed that they named their son Isaac—Laughter. It is unlikely they noticed the member of the household who was not laughing. Eliezer of Damascus, whose plans were so full of dreams and whose dreams were so full of plans, saw them all turned to dust by an outcome he had stopped considering as possible.

His companion in disappointment was named Joseph, who was also called Barsabbas and sometimes Justus. We meet him in the first chapter of the book of Acts as the followers of Jesus began to organize for whatever was coming now that the Christmas-to-Ascension story of the incarnation was completed. In their culture, twelve was a number that represented wholeness. God had given Israel twelve tribes, and Jesus had chosen twelve main disciples from among his followers. Before his ascension, Jesus commissioned them as witnesses to tell the gospel story throughout the world. With the defection and subsequent death of Judas Iscariot, they took steps to fill the twelfth position. It is significant that the criteria for consideration was one who had "accompanied us during all the time that the Lord Jesus went in and out among us, beginning from the baptism of John until the day he was taken up from us."

Of the one hundred twenty souls in the Christian community at that time, two men were able to meet that daunting standard: Justus and Matthias. Both had been faithful from start to finish, but were not included in the inner circle of disciples. Perhaps they helped distribute food during the feeding miracles, but they were not invited to the Last Supper. They withstood the harassment of the scribes and Pharisees, but were denied the private sessions with Jesus. They were steadfast at the cross, and still around for the resurrection. The loyalty of both men was exemplary, but only one would be given the title of apostle. The decision was made with the assumption that God can control that which is beyond human control, a literal roll of dice.

What went through the minds of the two men as the decision was made? They could not have been disinterested. Many people can live without exercising ambition, but everybody has at least a bit of it. Were they reluctant? Expectant? Hopeful? Doubtful? Planning their acceptance speech or picturing the look on their proud mother's face? There is no way to know, but when the results were known, Matthias was an apostle and Justus was back in the crowd. Is it too much to think that he was disappointed, even if he was also a little relieved? I think not. Can we assume he put on the brave face of the Not Chosen, congratulated Matthias, and left the room after a brief but decent interval? Probably so.

Eliezer and Justus are not mentioned in Scripture after these few words. Tradition tells us that Eliezer remained in the house of Abraham (what choice did he have?) and undertook the mission to find a bride for young Isaac. Justus is not mentioned again by any of his three names. We do not know how the two servants bore their disappointment, but by being Not Chosen they had a unique role to play in the future integrity of their community.

Almost every laudable family or institution claims to serve something greater than itself. Those chosen for leadership roles have distinct opportunities to serve that greatness by their stewardship. But only the Not Chosen can demonstrate the truth or untruth of the "serving something higher" ideal. If the disappointment of Eliezer and Justus took away their commitment, we would understand but we would not admire. But if, on the other hand, Eliezer continued to provide the kind of devoted service that raised him from household slave to majordomo, and if Justus continued as a loyal backbencher in the church, they elevated themselves and their community to new heights.

Anne Morrow Lindbergh was well acquainted with life's pain. In a letter to her mother, she once observed, "I do not believe that sheer suffering teaches. If suffering alone taught all the world would be wise since everyone suffers. To suffering must be added mourning, understanding, patience, love, openness and the willingness to remain vulnerable."[1] Eliezer and Justus, as well as all of us who feel the pain of the Not Chosen, have an opportunity to wend our way through Lindbergh's add-ons to suffering, hopefully coming out not only willing to remain vulnerable, but loyal and faithful as well. But no one can embody continuing vulnerability, faithfulness, and loyalty like the Not Chosen—if they choose to do so.

1. Anne Morrow Lindbergh, *Hour of Gold, Hour of Lead: Diaries and Letters of Anne Morrow Lindbergh, 1929-1932*, 3

14

Grasshoppers and Giants

Numbers 13–14

ONE OF THE MOST significant changes in history began when Joshua, Moses' successor, led the people of Israel into what they considered the promised land, launching a controversy that continues to this day. Most of us know the song if not the full story of the Battle of Jericho (Joshua 6), which began that long, ambiguous, and world-changing process. However, Numbers 13–14 describes the tense, soul searching days just before our spiritual ancestors took that fateful step. Those uncertain days of decision, poised as they were on the brink of either great fulfillment or great disaster, involved both the Israelites and those who already occupied the land. Fracking their story can shed light on our own struggles with change.

Behind them, the people of Israel had the multiple miracles of the Red Sea, manna in the wilderness, and water from the rock, as well as the golden calf and reluctance that bordered on rebellion. Their journey had been an arduous and contentious mixture of faith and failure, but every step was meant to bring them closer to the land they were convinced God was holding in trust for them. Before them was the door to that promised land. At that threshold, motivation turned into trepidation, and fresh doubts assailed them. Anyone who has laid hands on a long-sought diploma, welcomed a wished-for baby, or approached a long-deserved retirement can understand the disorientation that comes as dreams begin to morph into realities.

Moses selected proven and trusted men to scout the land. Their charge reads like a leader's worry list. Does the land look good? Are the people strong or weak? In other words, do we really want this place, and if so, can we take it? The first question proved easy to answer with a resounding "Yes!" The spies brought back a cluster of grapes so large that it took two men to carry them. It was so impressive that the image of two men carrying a cluster of grapes is the symbol of Israel's Department of Tourism to this day. The second question was far more problematic. The people in the land looked big—*really* big. They were, in fact, giants; the mythic Nephalim, the ancient equivalent of Vikings, Cossacks, and Comanches rolled into one. The Israeli spies felt as fragile as grasshoppers in their presence (Num 13:33). The group consensus was that Israel had no business taking them on. There is more to the story, but fracking allows us to take a slight detour at this point. The spies reported that they felt like insects, and that the occupants of the land regarded them the same way: no threat, but mere pests to be brushed off with the back of the hand.

From history's lofty perch, we can see that the grasshoppers were going to triumph over the giants, but no one on the ground could see that. The Israelites were frightened. The native people were overconfident. They were the descendants of giants, after all, secure in their fortified towns, unimpressed by the desert wanderers peering at them from a safe distance. There did not seem to be any way these ragamuffins could impact, much less overrun, a well-established and historically invincible people. Think of the way the Native Americans must have regarded the Pilgrims straggling ashore at Plymouth; or the attitude of mainline politicians who caught their first glimpse of Abraham Lincoln; or even our first impressions of snowy TV sets, clunky mobile phones, and fragile computers. How could those people, that man or those things possibly take over our lives? Those whose confidence is in the past are often unknowingly vulnerable to the future, just as those who are edging into the future are often knowingly intimidated by the past. For these reasons, the spies and the giants shared a common view: there was no way those grasshoppers could stand against those giants. Subsequent events proved that idea to be not only wrong, but completely backwards. It would take some time, but the grasshoppers would vanquish the giants.

None of that would have happened if the majority opinion of the spies had carried the day, but it did not. Caleb, one of the spies, spoke for advancing, but was shouted down by the others. Only Joshua, the man who would subsequently lead the advance, supported Caleb's view. The vote was two in favor and ten against. The people of Israel began packing for a return to Egypt. Moses and Aaron despaired to see their life's work crumbling before their eyes. The text tells us that God was ready to wash his hands of the whole project and, as in the past, Moses talked him out of it. With ten trusted and proven men quaking in their boots, the people preparing to retreat into the wilderness and an angry Yahweh ready to smite the lot of them, the great enterprise that is the foundation of our faith was in real danger of coming apart. Caleb and Joshua made a final pitch. The text tells us that God set a fatal illness on the ten frightened spies, an act which so impressed the people that they gathered their courage and resolved to follow through on their commitment to enter the land and face the giants.

That may be exactly what happened, and no one can be faulted for taking the story at face value. My personal experience, however, is that dissenting groups are seldom if ever neatly dispatched by strange diseases. I have not seen contrarians die as a group, but I have seen majority views die, and I have seen tides of group opinion reversed because of it. When a group consensus is motivated by fear of giants in one form or another, it can be reversed by an awareness of other giants more fearsome than the original ones. Fracking the drama in Numbers allows me to think it possible that Caleb raised the question of what it would be like to return to Egyptian slavery; what the people would be saying about themselves and their God if they turned back; what quitting at this point says about the people who sacrificed so much to come to this point; how turning back in fear makes a lie of everything they have done in faith. There was no escaping the fact that this was a defining moment. If they accepted the definition of themselves as grasshoppers, they would be grasshoppers forever. By whatever means—the death of the majority or the death of the majority view—our spiritual ancestors crossed the Jordon River and the rest, as they say, is history.

The drama in Numbers 13–14 is a classic confrontation between past and future, overconfidence and desperation. When giants peer out from behind walls of privilege or tradition, theology or constitutional guarantees, assumptions or mythologies, the opposition can look like grasshoppers. When ordinary people peer across the gaps of life at the security of giants, they can feel like grasshoppers. History, however, indicates that God has a special fondness for grasshoppers.

15

Purah and the Three Hundred

Judges 6–8

MUCH HAS BEEN WRITTEN about the responsibilities that rest on the shoulders of leaders in every walk of life (e.g., high priests), but little is said about the unique burdens borne by those who follow. That seems unfortunate, since there are far more followers than leaders in the world, and in hierarchical organizations, almost all leaders are following someone who ranks above them. Fracking the story of Gideon with an eye on his disciples offers an opportunity to consider the often-troubling issues of following.

Gideon's story is brief, worth reading, and not without humor. The text suggests that he would have been a difficult man to follow. He was a reluctant leader in constant need of elaborate assurances from God and given to strategies that swung between cravenly uncertain and dangerously bold. The biblical spotlight fell on him while he was threshing wheat secretly in his wine press for fear of the Midianites, fearsome desert dwellers who supplemented their diet by raiding the farms and fields of the Israelites. A messenger angel was required to provide an impressive flash of magic to convince Gideon to take action against Israel's enemies. Even then, his response was little more than vandalism of Baal's shrine carried out at night "because he was too afraid of his family and the townspeople to do it by day." Open rebellion had to wait for God to manipulate nature so outrageously that even Gideon was assured of divine favor. Once convinced, however, he became what a reasonable observer could only call reckless, albeit at God's direction. Facing an army of angry Midianites who were "thick as locusts," Gideon reduced his forces from twenty-two thousand to ten thousand, and then to a paltry three hundred. The upset victory sealed Gideon's place in Scripture, and his commendable obedience to God's plan lent his name to the distributors of hotel-room Bibles today.

His exploits involved ten servants who helped carry out the vandalism, a trusted retainer named Purah who joined his master in a midnight reconnaissance of the Midianite horde, and, of course, the three hundred brave souls who subsequently attacked them. Why did they choose to follow such an imperfect, erratic, and unpredictable man? The Bible does not tell us, but fracking can suggest possibilities.

Impoverished by the depredations of their unruly neighbors, the people of Israel were in dire straits. Crops and cattle nurtured in the thin soil of Israel went to feed marauding nomads, leaving hard-working Israelites with nothing but resentment. The locals were outnumbered, outmaneuvered, and outfought at every turn. Constant defeat naturally made fear the dominant reaction, which made hiding the chief defense. It was obvious that something had to be done and painfully obvious that no one was doing it. At least, that was true until the people woke one morning to find the Baal's altar desecrated. It was not any form of defiance toward the Midianites, but it was *something*; an appeal to deep memories of past glory, an act pointing to *the One* who freed their ancestors from slavery, a reminder of fragile hope glimmering in the darkness of despair. Somebody had to do something—and then somebody did! It was not a brave act, the perpetrator had to be ferreted out, and when he was revealed, few were impressed with his credentials. But at a time when nothing good was happening, Gideon did something defiant and challenging, and followers looking for a leader turned their eyes in his direction. A sense of dire necessity set in the context of paralyzed inaction can make the feeble gesture of an unlikely candidate very attractive.

When fed-up men like Purah looked at a flawed leader like Gideon in the light of even the dimmest glow of hope, they saw a man who did not fit the current mold of leaders, and their hearts rejoiced. The old style of leadership and its current practitioners had gotten the country into this mess, so a new style with a new face at least had the possibility of getting it out. Predictable leaders were adapting to problems, not fixing them. They were seeking better hiding places when they should have been seeking greater glory. Gideon at least was different: defiant, unpredictable, and therefore exciting. The horrified reaction of the village elders when they found the vandalized shrine to Baal was close enough to proof that Gideon just might be the man to break the log jam and lead them all to better days. So Purah and his friends cast their lot with Gideon.

Most people could see that Gideon was not up to the job. When the militia was called out to face the Midianites, he recklessly announced that the fearful could go home if they wanted to. Two-thirds of his army accepted the offer (Judges 7). This was followed by a seemingly arbitrary reduction in force based on how men drank from a stream. It was God's preparation for a miracle, but few if any would have known that. Even Gideon began to doubt his own tactics, and needed a midnight reconnaissance to bolster his faith in God's direction. Taking the faithful Purah with him, he crept to the edge of the Midianite camp and heard that they were more frightened than he was. Bolstered by that dose of relative courage, Gideon launched his attack and miraculously routed the enemy.

At this point, it is important to remember what we are exploring. This fracking exercise is about following, not about leading. Gideon's erratic leadership is in the Bible because it was a miracle. No case is being made for following unconventional people simply because they are unconventional. The footnotes of history are filled with stories of would-be Gideons who ended up in Midian meatgrinders. Jumping on their bandwagons, hoping or even expecting a Gideon-like miracle, is well short of wisdom. It is one thing to believe in miracles, and something quite different to rely on them.

But nonetheless, Purah and his companions joined in Gideon's cause. Our question is "Why?" At the beginning, it was the perception of necessity calling for something dramatically different from what had or had not been done before. In the following days, Gideon's behavior shook the foundations of reasonable confidence, yet Purah stayed on. His reasons may have been no more or less profound than the one given many centuries later by Peter when people were abandoning Jesus. Asked if he too was leaving, Peter replied, "To whom can we go?" (John 6:68). Purah, like Peter, stayed, because at that point there was no Plan B. They had cast their lot and had no real recourse. Peter affirmed Jesus as God's man. Purah did the same for Gideon. To seal the bargain, Purah's question was no longer one of choosing, but had become a matter of identity. He was more aware of his allegiance to his three hundred companions than to Gideon. He would not, could not, be the one to walk away from his community, no matter how frighteningly absurd the leader of that community might appear.

How and why leaders lead is a rich topic that is well and profitably explored. How and why followers follow is equally rich but rarely considered. Fracking the story of Purah can open an important door.

16

Jonathan and Jahzeil

Ezra 10:1–17

IN MANY WAYS, HUMAN communities are like the great herds of animals on the Serengeti Plain in Africa. We munch along quietly, maintaining our relationships and abiding by common standards. But occasionally something breaks into our equanimity and causes a stampede. Sometimes the reasons are good, as in times of danger from lions or belligerent nations. Often, they are baseless, like thunder or political fearmongering. In any case, for good reasons or bad, the stampede takes on a life of its own. Resistance may be brave and noble, but it is rarely successful. Perceptive wildebeests and thoughtful humans may rail against the mindless herd, but rational creatures hold little sway over those who have stopped thinking as Jonathan and Jahzeil can illustrate.

We meet these two in the book of Ezra during a pivotal but largely unnoticed period of our history: Jerusalem ca. 450 BCE. The book of Ezra and its companion piece, Nehemiah, are wonderful first-person accounts of leadership and perseverance in the face of incredible odds. On the physical level, they had the daunting task of rebuilding Jerusalem's walls and temple after the damage and neglect of what is called the Babylonian captivity, when the city's leaders were in exile. On the theological level, they had to figure out how God's people had erred and brought on the exile in the first place. Ezra the priest and Nehemiah the governor deserve nothing but accolades for their handling of the physical rebuilding. Christians are less enamored of their interpretation of what went wrong.

In this period, referred to as postexilic, Ezra, Nehemiah, and many others came to the conclusion that the contaminating sin of the Israelites was getting mixed up with non-Jews. The particular issue for Ezra was intermarriage. "The people of Israel, the priests and the Levites have not separated themselves from the peoples of the lands . . . They have taken some of the daughters as wives for themselves and for their sons. Thus, the holy seed has mixed itself with the peoples of the lands." The priest was horrified, and ordered not only an end to the practice but the termination of existing marriages to gentiles. The central point was that God expected his people to be pure and separated from the world. Others, including Jesus, took the opposite view, and commissioned the people of God to go into the world as witnesses, not out of it as quarantined exceptions. All of that was several centuries away; however, in Ezra's day, the people readily agreed with his separatist view, albeit with the practical request that it be done in an orderly manner and not while it was raining.

To understand the appeal of the separatist view, one must appreciate that our ancestors viewed sin and sinners the way we regard cancer cells. Rogue departures from God's way were considered the same way we judge rogue cells that contaminate the individual body. They must be cut out, or the body will die. No sympathy is accorded the living cancer cells or the foreign wives; no nostalgia for one's lung, breast, or family can take precedence over the radical process. So say modern oncologists and so said ancient theologians. The result of this in the fifth century BCE was a cultural stampede for purity that held sway for centuries, and is not without its adherents today.

Our point, however, is not the large question of the role of God's people, but the experience of those who set themselves over against the spooked herd. The text tells us that, in regard to the purging of gentile wives, only "Jonathan son of Asahel and Jahzeil son of Tikvah opposed this, and Meshullam and Shabbethai supported them." What was it like for them to stand against the herd, to oppose the majority? What is it like for anyone?

When the few stand against the many, our attention is naturally drawn to what is said and done. The more subtle but perhaps greater drama is out of view, in the hearts and minds of the contrarians. It is always important to know what one believes and, where possible, to know why one believes it. Such introspection plays a crucial role for those who stand against the majority. We must remember that the herd moves in the same way whether the cause is well- or ill-founded. Lions and thunder produce the same result. There is no guarantee, therefore, that opposition to or accord with the majority is either right or wrong.

This provides our first insight into Jonathan, Jahzeil, and company. They probably began by assuming the majority was correct, for the burden of proof must always be on the minority position. But something led them to make a U-turn, to look again at what was being said and realize that, at least by their calculations, things simply did not add up. Several centuries later, Peter would realize that "God shows no partiality, but everyone who fears him and does what is right is acceptable to him" (Acts 10:35). Did their opposition to Ezra's decree stand on such a lofty principle, or did they just happen to love their foreign wives too much to go along? We have no way of knowing, but opposition to a compelling majority can be rooted in either thought or feeling. Usually both.

The forces that move one to stand against the majority are seldom simple. Consider the motivations behind the dramatist Lillian Hellman's testimony during the McCarthy stampede in 1952: "I cannot and will not cut my conscience to fit this year's fashions"; or the abdication of King Edward VIII "for the woman I love"; or the loyal Anglican in the time of Oliver Cromwell, Sir Robert Shirley, "whose singular praise it was to have done the best of things in the worst of times"; or Quaker pacifists of the Greatest Generation; or Martin Luther King's *Letter from Birmingham Jail.* It does not matter how history regards these protesters. In their moment, they all have to begin with the majority, make a U-turn, and finally cast their lot with a minority view. Their reasons for taking such a risky position are almost always a blend of principle and personal preference. Difficult as it may be, marking the distinction between those two motivations is important for those who take such stands—and for those who judge them.

In addition to the difficult task of sorting through preference and principle, vocal minorities want to be alert to the temptations of the dark spirit of self-righteousness. Those in the majority face the same danger. Confidence can be falsely buoyed by group support, and Ezra propounds his view with far less than a wisp of humility. Our focus, however, is on the minority contrarians who stand against the stampeding herd. For them, the martyr's mantle can have its perverse appeal. Literature gives us two compelling expressions of such a mindset. Thomas Macauley's *Lays of Ancient Rome* celebrates the glory of losing in a noble cause.

> And how can man die better
> Than facing fearful odds,
> For the ashes of his fathers,
> And the temples of his Gods.

In the same vein, Thomas Becket's temptation in T. S. Eliot's *Murder in the Cathedral* makes martyrdom a perverse prayer by seeking to be the lowest on earth in order to become the highest in heaven. Such brave stances can become their own motivation by turning inevitable defeat into seemingly inevitable glory.

Why did Jonathan, Jahzeil, Meshullam, and Shabbethai stand against the persuasive powers of Ezra and the pervasive pressure of the majority? There is, of course, no way to know, but they and everyone who turns to face a stampede must also face themselves. To what degree are they following great principles, and to what degree might they be deifying personal preferences? Have they allowed their minority position to prematurely anoint them as martyrs? Such introspection is important and difficult in any circumstance, but especially so when the community herd is on the move

17

Simon and Caiaphas

Sirach 50:1–21; John 11:45–53

IT IS POSSIBLE THAT there are as many books about leadership as there are about love. The role is complex and full of the temptations, dangers, and rewards that characterize human life. The Bible includes famous examples such as Moses and David, determined ones like Ezra and Nehemiah, tragic figures like Saul and Samson, rebels like Absalom and Abimelech, and failures like Herod and Pilate, as well as the reluctant trailblazers Gideon and Jonah. Any and all of them would provide fruitful ground for fracking. With an admitted fondness for biblical paths less traveled, I would ask you to consider the leadership stories of the high priests of the Jerusalem temple, specifically Simon and Caiaphas. The latter is undoubtedly most famous because of his role in Holy Week, where Christian memory holds him in low esteem. Simon the high priest is not to be confused with Simon the principal disciple and apostle. This Simon served the temple in Jerusalem some two hundred years before the Christian story and is eulogized in the apocryphal Wisdom of Jesus Ben Sirach, otherwise known as Ecclesiasticus. Before fracking their stories, it may help to prepare the ground.

The temple in Jerusalem was the centerpiece of Jewish life, beginning with the first construction by Solomon in 957 BCE.

Its use, abuse, destruction, and rebuilding followed the ups and downs of Jewish history until the completion of what is called the second temple in 26 CE. This was the temple Jesus knew, and the one whose ruined Western Wall is a focal point for Jewish piety today. The presiding cleric in this vital institution was the high priest, whose office was hereditary and lifelong until the Roman occupation. Its origins could be traced to Aaron, the brother of Moses. The priestly office and the temple itself ended at the hands of the Romans in 70 CE. Our culture does not have an equivalent position with combined symbolic, theological, liturgical, and political power like that held by held by Simon and Caiaphas. Fracking may be the best way to enter their world and draw insight from their lives.

Simon is best known to us through the high praise of his eulogist, Jesus ben Sirach. In what is commonly referred to as Ecclesiasticus, the writer recounts the capital improvements made during Simon's term of office, bringing benefit not only to the temple precincts but to the citizens at large in the form of a large cistern. Then he turns to the man himself. His words defy summary:

> How glorious he was, surrounded by the people, as he came out of the house of the curtain.
>
> Like the morning star among the clouds, like the full moon at the festal season;
>
> like the sun shining on the temple of the Most High,
>
> like the rainbow gleaming in splendid clouds;
>
> like roses in the days of first fruits, like lilies by a spring of water,
>
> like a green shoot on Lebanon on a summer day;
>
> like fire and incense in the censer, like a vessel of hammered gold studded with all kinds of precious stones;
>
> like an olive tree laden with fruit, and like a cypress towering in the clouds.
>
> When he put on his glorious robe and clothed himself in perfect splendor, when he went up to the holy altar, he made the court of the sanctuary glorious.
>
> When he received the portions from the hands of the priests, as he stood by the hearth of the altar with a garland of brothers

around him, he was like a young cedar on Lebanon surrounded
by the trunks of palm trees. (Sir 50:5–12)

To say that Jesus ben Sirach was impressed by Simon as he led the
liturgies of the temple would be an understatement. Our focus,
however, is not on ben Sirach, but on Simon. How might he have
regarded himself in that role?

It is more than difficult to maintain the distinction between
the public role outside and the private person inside. Just as paint-
ers get paint on their hands and bakers get flour on their arms,
priests tend to get worship on themselves. Unlike paint and flour,
worship does not easily wash off at the end of the day. If ben Sirach saw Simon as a cedar surrounded by palm trees, can we fault
Simon if he sometimes felt like a cedar amid palms? Could he look
like a full moon when he stepped through the curtain if he did
not, at some level, think of himself that way? Did he, just before
he "came out of the house of the curtain," give his robe an extra
tug, smooth the hair over his ears, and enjoy the moment, like one
enjoys anticipating a sip of fine wine? Of course, we have no way
of knowing, but we have reasonable ways of guessing. People who
are good at what they do usually enjoy doing it. But did that enjoy-
ment confine itself to liturgy? Did his public persona carry over
into his home life, making him arrogant and pompous? Did he
let his hair down with his friends, or were they simply a garland
around him? Did he give one the time of day in the same sonorous
tones he used to pronounce a blessing?

For Simon's sake, if not for those who shared life with him, I
hope not. No one is made to *be* high priest or high anything. We
are all made as fallible human beings. That fallibility is intended
to remind us that we are incomplete and dependent on God and
one another. When we forget that fact, we become counter to our
creation, and embark on a lonely journey through life, a journey of
pretense instead of authenticity, of role instead of relationship. We
do have roles to play, and some of them, especially public leadership ones, are seductive and can lure us away from our common
humanity. In this regard, public leaders like clergy, politicians,

performers, teachers, and military officers share a common bond and a common temptation with Simon the High Priest.

Caiaphas undoubtedly had the same liturgical responsibilities as Simon, but we have no information about how he fulfilled that role. We only know him as a politician, a role that circumstances made somewhere between impossible and inconceivable. Traditional Christian memory usually overlooks that fact in its universal condemnation of Caiaphas for being the man who engineered the crucifixion of Jesus. Before fracking his story, it will be worth our time to consider the circumstances in which it took place.

Caiaphas served eighteen years as high priest, substantially longer than any others during the Roman occupation, a fact that establishes his diplomatic skills if not his spiritual development. The times were complex and troubled. The occupiers were fierce enforcers of the *Pax Romana,* namely peace on Rome's terms alone. Their response to unrest in any form was swift, efficient, cruel, and complete. The Jewish people were argumentative by nature, disdainful of pagans in general and Romans in particular. Their chaffing under the Roman yoke was exacerbated by anticipation of a God-given deliverer (the messiah or anointed one) and the memory of a successful rebellion against the Greeks in the previous century. Confident of God's support, they were ready for rebellion.

If one could have had a satellite view of Jerusalem in the days before Holy Week that year, the scene would have been a perfect storm brewing. Disciplined Roman Legions were marching south from their base at Caesarea to reinforce the garrison in Jerusalem. From all directions, pious, patriotic Jews were streaming into the city for the annual observance of Passover, God's miraculous deliverance of the Israelites from Egyptian slavery. East of the city in Bethany, Jesus and his followers were gathering the messianic symbols designed to excite and possibly ignite the crowds. The eye of the storm was the temple, where the high priest and his advisors sweated and fretted about the potential for violence. That threat was certainly not imagined, and would become a reality in 70 CE when the conflict did break out, only to be swiftly crushed by Romans who, in the process, destroyed the temple and scattered the people so thoroughly they did not reconvene until 1948 CE, nearly two thousand years later.

The traditional Christian view of Caiaphas is that of an orthodox protector who was afraid of new ideas, allergic to new truth, and immune to insight. This comes largely from the depiction of him in the book of Acts, where he led an active suppression of the early Christians. If that is an accurate representation of the high priest, it certainly does not make him unique among institutional leaders, although it can be noted in passing that the Christian memory of Caiaphas was not likely to be positive. Oppressed people rarely if ever impute noble or even logical motives to their oppressors. No matter what Caiaphas's true colors might have been, he did the only thing he could have done with the information he had at the time.

The high priest was by definition a politician bearing responsibility for decisions that affected the lives of many. Most of us have a narrow understanding of "politician" which allows us to distance ourselves from them. But anyone with responsibilities that affect others is in fact a politician, whether the arena is government, church, family, or corporate or community life. With that wider perspective, all of us can recognize the politician's inability to please all of the people all of the time; the frustration of making adequate decisions with inadequate information; and the necessity of requiring some to make sacrifices for others. That is what must be done, whether the arena is the world or the playground, or somewhere in between.

John's Gospel tells us that Caiaphas urged Jesus' crucifixion by pointing out that it was better to have one man suffer than the whole nation perish. That is a painfully reasonable conclusion if one were convinced the whole nation was about to suffer. I would suggest that the high priest and his advisors were convinced of that point, and that their thinking was not without evidence to support it. Jesus' Messianic claim, acted out so dramatically on Palm Sunday, lit the fuse on Jerusalem's Passover powder keg. Nobody from the man in the street to the men in the temple doubted that he intended to lead an armed rebellion. The decision to crucify him was a decision to prevent an explosion by cutting the fuse. I must say that while I hate that decision, if I had the information and concerns the high priest and his advisors had, I would have agreed.

Once made, the decision was swiftly carried out: a nighttime arrest to avoid public scrutiny; a hasty trial to beat the Passover deadline; a political threat to the fragile Roman governor to get a legal death sentence; manipulation of an excitable crowd to simulate popular support before a pious return to matters of temple liturgy while rough-hewn soldiers carried out the untidy details.

One of Good Friday's most popular hymns is "Were You There?" which asks us to see ourselves as part of the crucifixion. Fracking the story of the High Priest Caiaphas adds some dimensions to that wonderful hymn. If we have ever had what amounts to a political position which made us responsible for decisions that affect the lives of others . . . and if what we knew at the time made it impossible for us to please everybody while satisfying every moral principle . . . and if we knew that by bending the truth just a little we could avoid great consequences not only for ourselves but for others . . . and if we have ever done what we thought was best even if it was not perfect . . . then the answer must be *"Yes"*: *we were there when they crucified our Lord.*

18

Miracle Workers

Luke 21:1–4; John 6:1–14; John 2:1–11

THOSE WHO SUPPLY RAW material for the acts of God are often unaware of the role they are playing. There is no way the poor widow who caught Jesus' attention as she placed her mite in the temple treasury could have imagined the generosity her gift would leverage in the future. It is highly unlikely she even noticed the man who was so moved by her example that he told her story to his followers. It is doubtful she considered herself an example at all. She was just doing what she had always done. While Jesus was expounding on her stewardship, she probably left the temple, picked up a loaf bread and a quart of milk on the way home, fed the cat, and went to bed. She never knew that, like Helen of Troy, she had just launched a thousand ships of charity and relief. The act was the widow's, but the action was all God's.

God's miracles are often like that. Most of us have experienced unintentional gestures and casual words that have had profound impacts on our lives. Role models do not often think of themselves as such; real heroes usually have to be told how their actions are regarded; preachers are often thanked for addressing something when they had no idea they were doing so. Of course, the devil uses those instances as well. Great damage has been done without any intention or knowledge. We have all been puzzled by the offense or injury people trace to something we have said or done innocently. God has no monopoly on the technique, but it is a favorite, and one that fracking allows us to explore.

Consider the familiar story of Jesus feeding the multitudes. All four Gospels record such an event, with Mark and Matthew indicating that it happened twice. The working of the miracle itself is difficult nail down. The humanist perspective suggests that Jesus inspired generosity in the crowd and led people to share what they had tucked away in their sleeves. The spiritual view recognizes the parallel with God's creative powers in Genesis. Pursuing those and other routes of interpretation are safely in the hands of biblical scholars. Fracking takes a different turn and focuses on John's account (John 6:1–14), which tells us that when Jesus suggested feeding the multitude, the disciple Andrew noted that "There is a boy here who has five barley loaves and two fish." Fracking allows us to wonder why this young man would have so much food with him in the first place and what role he might have played in the ensuing miracle.

I can see only two possibilities for his abundant supply. One is personal, the other commercial. He may have had a prodigious appetite and intended to eat it all himself, or he intended to sell it. The first possibility seems unlikely even for a teenager. The second has more credibility. One can imagine his parents, hearing that Jesus was in the area and aware of his popularity, saw the marketing potential in the crowds that followed him. Mother set about baking barley loaves while father went to the lake for fish. When all was ready, their son was dispatched to sell them when the crowd got hungry. They might have been the first, but they were certainly not the last to see the economic potential around Jesus.

Fracking suggests that the boy was in the crowd for economic rather than spiritual purposes. To be more precise, he was there because his parents sent him. If that is the case, in all probability Andrew paid him for the merchandise and, his task completed, the young man went home. His motivations were understandable and decent. He was obeying his parents, and presumably asked a fair price for his goods. But his motivations were also narrow. Once they were fulfilled, his interest in the larger process around him waned so he missed the miracle that Christ wrought with the food he provided. Throughout history, reasonable and honorable (but tightly focused) people like this young man have been walking away from miracles, their eyes on human currency instead of God's.

The wedding at Cana provides another illustration of people working with the raw material of God's actions, but perhaps missing the finished product. As the familiar story unfolds, a wedding reception ran out of wine. Jesus' mother basically tricked him into doing something about the problem. Jesus' intervention was substantial, as he produced about one hundred fifty gallons of what the sommelier called "the good wine," better than that originally chosen for the party. John tells us that no one knew where it came from, "though the servants who had drawn the water knew." But what did they know?

I think they knew who was behind the new wine. I doubt they knew why or how. Like the widow in the temple and the boy with the loaves and fish, they did what they were supposed to do. One of the wedding guests told them to fill six large jars with water, then take a cup of it to the caterer. They did so, but it is unlikely they were aware of much of anything beyond the verbal instructions and the physical actions. In this regard, they were like the blind man Jesus would later heal at the Pool of Siloam in Jerusalem (John 9:1–41). When the authorities asked the man how he had been healed, he could only tell them that Jesus made mud, put it on his eyes, and told him to wash it off in the pool. When he did, he could see. He had no idea why Jesus would have done such a thing, or how those steps might have cured his blindness. The servants at the wedding would have been similarly limited.

The deeper interpretations and wider implications of God's actions are not always, or even often, readily apparent. Time, experience and reflection are the litmus tests by which we recognize God's activity in the world. The raw material for that activity is often provided unknowingly without the test results. It seems worth noting that the suppliers in these stories were simply doing what they were supposed to be doing. The acts were theirs, but the action was God's. The fulfillment of God's actions in the world does not depend on human will, or even human willingness, for fulfillment.

19

Bartimaeus

Mark 10:46–52

WHY IS IT THAT euphoria can vanish so quickly, leaving little more than a vaguely embarrassing hint of remembrance? We know that emotional excitement is a fragile vessel, easily swamped by other realities. But why? The Gospels of Matthew, Mark, and Luke all tell a story that may shed light on that question. Mark is the one who gives us a name and adds some cogent details, so it is the best one for fracking.

The story is of Bartimaeus, a blind man in Jericho panhandling beside the Jerusalem Road. Hearing a larger-than-usual crowd approach, he asked the reason for it, and learned that Jesus was passing on his way to Jerusalem. Recognizing his chance, Bartimaeus began to cry out for mercy, and kept it up in spite of stern warnings to mind his manners. He made such a racket that Jesus heard him and healed him. We are told that Bartimaeus "regained his sight and followed [Jesus] on the way." It is a wonderful story until one begins to wonder what happened after that. Bartimaeus is not mentioned again. How long did he follow Jesus? Did he continue as a lifelong disciple, or did his enthusiasm fade? Was he there at the cross? Did he stay for the resurrection? Did he experience Pentecost? There is, of course, no record, and no way to know. There are, however, some possibilities to consider.

Before Jesus came by, Bartimaeus was a beggar who sat on his cloak day after day, asking for alms whenever his ears told him someone was near enough to lay a coin on his upstretched palm. His world was confined to a harsh simplicity: ask often, receive seldom. His role in society was to keep his discomfort from making others uncomfortable. Nothing more was asked of him. His spiritual life mirrored his economic one: ask often, receive seldom. He prayed for healing, but doubted it would ever come. He knew it was unwise to rail against God, just as it was unwise to overly share his hard story with those around him. The prevailing theology told him that he was being punished by God, and experience told him that he was being ignored by the community. He was beyond marginalized. All he had was his cloak, which served as his office where he spent his days, as his bank where tossed coins were collected, and as his blanket that kept him warm at night. To the world that passed by, he was literally an invalid, not valid, neither usable nor compelling. It was a small world, unadorned by respect or affection. The hopeless surface of his life hid a seething resentment underneath.

The dismissive attitude of society found voice in the response of the crowd to his cries for mercy when "many sternly ordered him to be quiet." There was no place for someone like Bartimaeus while real valid life was passing by. But Jesus had a different idea about what life is all about. Remember that he was on his way to Jerusalem to drink from the bitter cup we know as Holy Week. It must have been an absorbing prospect for Jesus, as his prayer in Gethsemane indicates, yet he stopped and faced the blind man who was storming the walls of propriety with his great need. When Jesus turned to face him, Bartimaeus did a most extraordinary thing. Mark tells that he threw off his cloak and stepped forward. His cloak was his world, his base, his thin comfort on a cold night in a cold world. Yet he threw it off the way children throw off blankets on Christmas morning or the way rockets throw off boosters when they reach outer space. If Jesus did not heal him, how would he ever find his cloak again? Bartimaeus was betting it all on what would transpire in the next few moments

The confrontation between them was short. Jesus asked the simplest of questions: "What do you want me to do for you?" "Let me see again," said Bartimaeus. "Go," said Jesus, "your faith has made you well." The cure was immediate, and the joyful former invalid followed Jesus.

But he did not follow him very far. One reason is simply physical. Jerusalem is fifteen miles from Jericho, and over three thousand feet higher. The road is long and steep, hard on the strongest legs, but impossible when one has been sitting for several years. Bartimaeus's sight was restored, but not his youthful vigor. He missed the events of Holy Week because he could not keep up even if he wanted to. But there were other realities that took him away from following his healer.

Euphoria is subject to complicating realities. Weddings become marriages, college life turns into a career track, pregnancies lead to parenthood, even retirement requires a reorientation of priorities. For Bartimaeus, the harsh simplicity of his old "ask often and receive seldom" world was placed on a new axis. No longer a blind beggar, he would have to join the workforce. His economy shifted from alms to wages. He now had the actual demand as well as the potential satisfaction of earning his way. Would the people who supported him when he was asking for alms respond to him when he was asking for work? His previous role in society had been to keep quiet. Now he had a voice. How did he use it? He had lived, worked, eaten, and slept on his cloak, but now the cloak was gone, and each of those activities required new arrangements.

His family had to be considered. They were the ones who left him to eke out his survival on the Jerusalem Road. Should he return to their fold? Would they want him? Would he want them? Forgiveness had never been a possibility before. Was it now a necessity?

His relationship with God was also challenged, if not changed. Bartimaeus found as others have that when counting blessings, it makes a big difference when you start the count. Does his attitude toward God begin afresh after the healing, or can it include the time of blind begging? Was God now to be regarded as merciful and good after years of ignoring him? Before Jesus, he had ample justification for anger. Could he simply turn, literally repent of a view that continued to make sense, even if circumstances had changed? New worlds even long-sought after ones like healing, present realities and challenges that are difficult to anticipate. The business of seeking is unlike the stewardship of something found. Bartimaeus's long and possibly impatient wait for the restoration of his sight ill prepared him for all that seeing involves. There is no question about whether it is better to see or to be blind, but each is its own world with demands, tasks, and compensations that are not found in the other. His reaction to Jesus was euphoria—brief joy—but a precursor to other realities.

20

Herod and Pilate

Mark 6:21–28; John 18:28—19:16

EVERY RELIGION, CULTURE, AND country treasures the examples of its martyrs. Those who give their lives for great principles, communities, and goals bear "witness" (the literal meaning of martyr) to what is best in human nature. They are role models for us all as we face the many small sacrifices of day-to-day living. Their stories are told and retold to great advantage all around the world. There is another group, however, widely present in every religion, culture, and country who are the opposite of martyred heroes. In spite of their omnipresence, we lack a word to describe them, perhaps because we do not like speaking of them, which limits our capacity to learn from their poor examples. If a new term can be coined, I suggest we call these people anti-martyrs. Unlike those who sacrifice themselves for great causes like God, country, or comrades, anti-martyrs sacrifice *someone else* to serve *small* causes like ego, career, or social standing. Anti-martyrs and their victims are easily found on corporate ladders, in gossip sessions, and more than a few romances. In the Christian story, it is worth noting that the first and greatest martyrs, John the Baptist and Jesus, were sacrificed by infamous anti-martyrs who were serving narrow and unworthy causes. Fracking the stories of Herod Antipas and Pontius

Pilate can provide insight into the anti-martyr approach to life that is so widespread but so seldom mentioned.

History records that King Herod's family were devout monotheists. Unfortunately, their one god was power. Acquiring, maintaining, and expanding political power was the principal function of this completely dysfunctional family. Intrigue, lies, shifting alliances, and various forms of murder were their only constants. The Gospel of Matthew tells us that the king's father, Herod the Great, killed all of the young children of Bethlehem in response to the suggestion of the Magi that a possible competitor had been born there. While that event is uncorroborated by other sources, there is an abundance of evidence that makes the story psychologically consistent with the family obsession with power. Fracking the account of the martyrdom of John the Baptist must concentrate on Antipas and his family's worship of power.

John was no real threat to the king or his household, but he was critical of them. Herod, while married to an Arabian princess, met and fell in love with his half-brother Philip's wife, Herodias. They each divorced their spouses and were married. Significantly, Herodias maintained custody of her daughter Salome and brought the girl along to their new home. Such divorcing and remarrying was an appalling violation of both Scripture and custom, according to the unyielding principles of John the Baptist. With his well-known lack of subtlety, the prophet named the royal couple as adulterers. Herod was not so much offended as fascinated. That kind of steel-edged morality was an anomaly in the king's world, bordering on cross-cultural in its strangeness. Antipas was Jewish and knew both Judaic tenets and the enthusiasm of some of its adherents, but John was different. He took his beliefs right to the palace and into the king's bedroom. One would have to be crazy to do that, but John was not crazy. He was on fire with something Herod had never seen burn, a power he had yet to experience, much less exploit. John had to be arrested, of course; there was no room for such overt criticism in an absolute monarchy. But the king was intrigued as he listened to the angry prophet. He was not interested in John's logic or his rhetoric—it was the power behind them that was so compelling. In a strange way, the absolute authority of John's God of Law had something Herod's god of power lacked. The effect on the king was enticing and disturbing. He was not through wondering about the baptizer, but his wife was. It was embarrassing enough to have that wild man stirring up the rabble, but when he began to get the king's ear, it became serious. It was obvious to her that, like any anti-martyr, her husband would discard her like an out-of-fashion garment if she became inconvenient. Herodias had no intention of letting that happen.

While she had not known her husband long, she knew him well. The queen had noticed that what the king liked best about having power was the slack-jawed admiration of those around him as he exercised it. He loved to pass judgement with a flick of his finger, grant favors with a nod of his head, and create mandates with idle thoughts, but people had to see it done for it to be satisfying. That simple fact made him pathetically dependent on applause. It was his kryptonite, his Achilles heel, the single vulnerability he could not defend. Herodias had only to play on that weakness and the danger of John the Baptist could be removed.

The king's birthday provided the perfect stage. His regular toadies would be there, along with representatives of many monarchs whose job was to send abroad reports on Herod's strengths and weaknesses. The perfect foil was the doe-eyed Salome, Herodias's daughter from her first marriage. Among Herod's vanities was an eye for young ladies and a need to have them swoon as he preened and strutted his kingly power. The mother was sure her daughter could bring the monarch to the brink of foolishness.

The party was in full swing. Wine flowed freely, and ribald humor did its magic to lower community standards. Salome danced before the king and his guests. As the saying goes, it did not take long for Herod's temperature to rise above his IQ. "Ask me whatever you wish," he shouted, "and I will give it!" His likely expectation that he could demonstrate his magnificence by granting her a shiny jewel or a silk cape was dashed when, after a conversation with her mother, she replied, "I want you to give me the head of John the Baptist on a platter." Silence fell on the gathering like a lid on a boiling pot. Every conversation stopped, every eye was on the king, every ear cocked for his reply. They all knew of Herod's fascination with John. They could see it on the king's face. The king could see wicked expectation all around him. The chilling specter of humiliation was close at hand. Even though it was only a few seconds, the pause seemed way too long before his head nodded slightly and John's fate was sealed. The party never quite regained its momentum after that, and the evening was cut short.

Herod Antipas was a perfect anti-martyr: self-centered while pretending to be magnanimous; weak while appearing strong; cowardly behind self-awarded medals; dependent while feigning sovereignty. His ego was so fragile and precious that no sacrifice to protect it was too great, as long as someone else made the sacrifice.

Pontius Pilate shared Herod's anti-martyr principle of self before others, but the context of his story allows fracking to explore different possibilities. Pilate's arena was not that of absolute executive, but a senior officer in what later empires would call the Colonial Office. There was a bureaucracy to take into account and an emperor who could not be ignored. The Roman Empire was full of complexities, but its purpose was remarkably simple. The far-flung colonies were to provide a steady flow of goods and services to the center which was Rome. The standard carried by its legions said simply SPQR: "The Senate and People of Rome." There was no missionary zeal or cultural pretension to complicate the basic mission. Roman administrators were to maintain that flow and avoid disruption at all costs.

Although Pilate had risen to the enviable rank of governor, it is unlikely that any of his peers coveted his assignment to Judea. The population was fractious, troublesome, and given to rebellion; the weather was oppressive, the terrain uninviting. Judea had little to contribute to the empire's purpose or wealth other than its geographic link to more prosperous colonies. Since the main task of the Judean governor was to see that something bad did not happen, the job was thankless; successes were unnoticed, failures were writ large. The only thing Pilate had in common with his charges was mutual contempt. It was not anyone's idea of a "dream job."

The best one could hope for was an uneventful tour and a better posting afterwards.

Roman governors lived in Caesarea, a gentile city on the breezy Mediterranean coast, fifty satisfying miles away from the hostile energy of Jerusalem. Pilate, like his predecessors, went to the Holy City for Passover as a matter of duty, to keep a firm hand on that annual concentration of patriotic memory and religious fervor. History remembers that things did not go well, but it is unlikely that Pilate ever knew his anti-martyr indecision would, in modern terms, go viral.

Shortly after arriving in Jerusalem, the temple leadership presented the governor with a demand. There was a man who was problematic to their faith, and they wanted him executed, a step only Pilate could take. Seeing no reason to get caught up in Jewish controversies, Pilate declined. The high priest upped the ante and insisted that the man wanted to be king. Historians have wondered why Pilate did not send Jesus to the cross at that moment, since there was a creditable charge of treason. Fracking suggests a possibility.

Pilate saw the situation as a test of will and authority. If he gave in to this demand of the priests, where would it stop? He had to show them he was not willing to be pushed around by their hysterical reaction to the delusions of some up-country bumpkin. To Pilate, the issue was authority, and he chose to take a firm stand. That stance, however, soon lost its certainty. The governor had not heard Jesus' story about a house built on sand that could not withstand the rain and wind (Matt 7:24–27), but he found himself living in one nonetheless. The temple authorities continued to prattle on and hit on the notion that Jesus said he was the Son of God.

Pilate was no one's idea of a religious man, but he accepted the prevailing wisdom that the gods were real and one does what one can to avoid crossing them. The possibility that Jesus was somehow connected to that reality was frightening. As his brows were still furrowed over that point, his wife sent word that she had had a troubling dream about Jesus' innocence (Matt 27:19). While a little resentful of the fact that his wife could take a nap while he was dealing with these problems, he still knew that believers said the gods often spoke through dreams. Perhaps his firm stance was not on firm ground. He had the man brought before him. He was not impressed. There was no revolutionary ardor about him, just the naïve righteousness that characterizes dreamers and the arrogant contempt that characterizes defeated people in occupied countries. Surely the Jerusalem crowds would identify with those qualities and support Pilate's opposition to the temple's pressure. But it was not to be. To top it off, the priests piously pointed out that *they* had no king but Caesar, cleverly implying that Pilate may not be so loyal. Now his career was in danger, to say nothing of his neck. The only thing left for the Roman governor to do was cut his losses and preserve what was left of his dignity. He publicly washed his hands of the whole thing and tossed What's-His-Name to the wolves.

To Pilate, it was a minor skirmish in the larger war of authority, career, and ego. As with so many anti-martyrs, his perception was exactly backwards. History has determined that authority, career, and ego are minor considerations amid the larger issues of truth, justice, and fidelity.

Martyrs can inspire us. Anti-martyrs can make us think.